HOW TO CATCH A FROG

HOW TO CATCH A FROG

and other stories of
family, love, dysfunction,
survival, and DIY

Heather Ross

STC CRAFT | A MELANIE FALICK BOOK

STEWART, TABORI & CHANG | NEW YORK

Published in 2014 by Stewart, Tabori & Chang
An imprint of ABRAMS.

Text copyright © 2014

Library of Congress Control Number: 2013945657
ISBN: 978-1-61769-098-3

Editor: Melanie Falick
Designer: Brooke Reynolds for inchmark
Production Manager: Erin Vandeveer

The text of this book was composed in Fournier.
Printed and bound in the United States.

10 9 8 7 6 5 4 3 2 1

Stewart, Tabori & Chang books are available at special discounts when
purchased in quantity for premiums and promotions as well as fundraising
or educational use. Special editions can also be created to specification.
For details, contact specialsales@abramsbooks.com or the address below.

115 West 18th Street
New York, NY 10011
www.abramsbooks.com

For my mother and my daughter,
and for Mike and Jane

contents

Prologue 8

How to Make a Teepee From Plastic Flowers 10

How to Make Paper Flowers 21

How to Make Coffee Logs to Start a Fire 33

How to Make a Bonfire 44

How to Catch a Frog 57

How to Save a Drowning Child (Part I) 68

How to Help a Bird Build a Nest 76

How to Make a Warm Bed 90

How to Swim a Horse 100

How to Make Cream of Broccoli Soup 109

How to Make a Very Warm Pair of Pants 120

How to Run Away 138

How to Fend Off a Bear 147

How to Start a Children's Clothing Company 158

How to Make Sugar on Snow 168

How to Save a Drowning Child (Part II) 182

How to Eat Fresh Trout 195

How to Begin Again 202

How to Have Faith 210

How to Not Turn Into Your Mother 217

How to Make a Home 230

Acknowledgments 239

prologue

I COME FROM A FAMILY OF DREAMERS.

My grandfather bought the land in Vermont, the place that would define my family and my upbringing, in the early 1960s. It was almost a thousand acres, mostly mountaintop, with a few dilapidated farmhouses and outbuildings. Much of it had been worked as dairy farms for more than a century before my family arrived, and because it had been grazed by cows for so many decades, it was still full of high green meadows and clear, breathtaking views into the valleys below.

My grandfather had originally intended to build a country house there, in the style of homes he had admired when he lived and worked in Austria and Switzerland—a grand, chalet-style place where his four children, who had grown up mostly apart, in separate boarding schools, could spend their summers. He longed to be the head of a large, close family at least in part, I believe, to make up for what he thought was missing from his own upbringing. His childhood had come apart when he was a little boy, when his father died and his mother remarried, and he was sent away to live with relatives. While he had become very successful financially and now had a family of his own, they still did not have a singular place to call home. His was a grand and ambitious vision of a place where they would become close and be together for generations to come. His children, however, had other plans, largely inspired by the political and cultural shifts of that era. Instead, it became a place where each of them would stake a claim, two as permanent residents and two as itinerant, seasonal visitors, each by then so independently formed, so formal and competitive with one another, that there was little hope that they would ever develop the sort of bonds that my grandfather had longed for. It was a place, dramatic and vast, remote and private, and a time, tumultuous and inspired, where anything could be imagined.

My mother and father were married in 1969, and moved into one of the old farmhouses while building their own geodesic dome on the hillside site they had been given as a wedding gift. In an old cowshed next to the house, they kept a herd of five goats, including a big white dam named Cassie who produced such amazing amounts of milk that she won blue ribbons at state fairs. A neighboring farmer gave her to my parents because he couldn't keep her out of his gardens, even when he surrounded them with barbed wire. One morning, he was so angry that he put her in the back of his truck and drove her to my parents, who had just learned that they were expecting twins. My sister and I were born in November, during a blizzard. When we were just six weeks old my mother, exhausted from nursing two babies, closed her bedroom door for three days and slept. My father, having no access to or money for formula, filled glass baby bottles with milk from Cassie's udders. Cassie's diet was grass in the summer and hay in the winter, cut from the fields around us that were not planted, but left to grow thick with weeds, wild-flowers, goldenrod, and ragweed.

My first food, then, was made of this place—of weeds and of dreams.

HOW TO
make a teepee
from plastic flowers

 THE TROUBLE WITH MAKING A BEANPOLE
teepee is that summer usually ends before all the
beans reach the top, or that the beans stop reaching
for the top before summer ends. You can trick a
sunflower by putting a paper bag over its head for
a few hours out of the day; it will think that it's in
the shadow of another sunflower, and it will try
to become bigger and taller. But you must always
take the bag off by noon, because if it doesn't get any sun at
all, it will simply give up, and it will lie down, with its flower
still facing the sky, which is far too sad a sight for summertime.
Beans, however, once comfortably stretched out on a net of
sticks and string, tilted toward the sun, will get sleepy and thick
but will have no reason to continue to reach.

The other trouble with a beanpole teepee is that nothing
grows beneath it. You will wait all summer long, which for a
child is both a lifetime and an instant, and then you will crawl
inside and find it to be unexpectedly dark and damp. You will
feel the cold wet on your knees through your jeans before you
are even all the way inside because you have watered it so many
times, hoping to make it grow thick and tall, that the earth inside

will be almost black with mud. You will drag in a towel or a blanket or something else, but that too will eventually feel wet, and then you will not want to go back into your beanpole teepee, and you will forget that you left some of your favorite things inside it when you went there on the longest day of the year, before its days became numbered.

This is why you should make a teepee out of plastic flowers. I know you must think I am very tacky, or very lazy, but here is what I can promise you: that when you are finished and you crawl through the opening and into your small house, you will feel whole, and satisfied, and your mind will be settled. To make anything by hand, whether it is to feed or to warm or to shelter yourself, to succeed in meeting some small—or not small—need that exists within us, this is what we and every other thing with a heart that walks this earth are meant to do with our hands and with our days. And when you are inside a structure that you have built yourself, whether your walls are made of plastic or grass or brick or beans, you will be at home.

I know this because, when I was a child, I lived on land inhabited by people who lived in houses that they had built for themselves, by hand. The only thing that these three houses had in common, apart from their rural route delivery address, was that they were built without a working knowledge of architecture or construction. All three houses, plus a century-old farmhouse that we all called The Red House, were within distant sight of each other, along the last half mile of a narrow dirt road that climbed into the mountains, growing narrower and grassier and eventually becoming a simple trail that could easily be lost before it disappeared completely into the woods.

The smallest house, and the first house that you would drive past, belonged to Donald Combs. The mountaintop was owned by my maternal grandfather, who had bought it from the Combs family, who had been there for a very long time. One of the conditions of the sale was that the family's youngest son, Donald, could stay in the small house that he had built for himself. Buying land in northern Vermont can be tricky.

We were told that Donald had been in his mother's belly when she was washing the dinner dishes, one night long ago. She had both of her hands in the water when the house was struck by a ball of lightning that had come rolling down the side of the mountain, and the water in the sink became electrified, causing Mrs. Combs to be thrown clear across the room and against the wall. She had recovered, but Donald was not like her other children, and she blamed the lightning ball.

When the processes of operation on small dairy farms were modernized in the early 1960s, mountaintop farms like the Combses' could no longer survive. Donald's extended family packed up and moved onward, to the Midwest, but Donald did not want to go anywhere. According to my grandfather, who arrived to pay for the land in cash and found the Combs family waiting for him, their cars and trucks heavily packed, Donald did not seem sad to see them go and waved them on, standing barefoot in a soft, cool patch of clover and buttercups, more than six feet tall and thin as a green bean and with the wide, excited smile of a child. When they were gone, he walked back to his little two-room house, which was made of plywood and tin and had a dirt floor. There was no running water or electricity; he had a small, black wood-burning cookstove that had a single-burner plate, and there was an outhouse that sat just downhill, at the bottom of a trail through thick green brush. In every season but winter, we would make an unsupervised pilgrimage to his house almost every day, where he would welcome us in with a broad, gappy smile, and give us silver coins and bottle caps and bent nails, and tell us that we were beautiful girls. We understood that Donald was different, and special, and harmless, and kind. When we had a wasp's nest that needed to be taken down or a raccoon that needed to be intimidated, one of us would be sent to get Donald. He would walk back home with us, always barefoot, with his shotgun over his shoulder.

Donald also liked to talk. He wasn't much of a conversationalist, just more of a talker. You could get stuck for hours if you slowed down in front of his house and he saw you in time to get in front of your car. Sometimes his fly was wide open. He wore clothing that looked to have been army issue, with his pants always slightly too short, sitting just above his narrow ankles and broad, long feet. He was barefoot by choice or habit, sometimes even when there was snow on the ground, and even when he was chopping firewood, and we made a game of counting his toes each spring. The number changed enough to keep things interesting. He was already an old man when we knew him as children, and had lost nearly all of his teeth. A family friend, a young woman who loved my uncle, took him into town one summer and bought him a set of teeth, and afterward he smiled even wider. When Donald, at a very old age, died peacefully in his sleep, there were over a hundred people at the wake, an event that was a silent, reverent testament to a man who had not hurt or angered, or even bested, a single person in his long lifetime, and had not made a single enemy. His life had been solitary and self-sufficient, and he had lived almost all of it in that small tin shack.

The house that my parents built could be seen from the road just past Donald's place, but you had to park and walk up the hill, through a pasture, to reach it. Theirs was a geodesic dome based on Buckminster Fuller's designs. It was a brave thing to do, especially considering the building site, which was at the top of the mountain surrounded by a thousand acres of wilderness in northern Vermont, with nothing but dairy farms and small towns for fifty miles in every direction beyond. I remember little, but I do recall very clearly the feeling of waking up inside that huge space, which was not divided by walls, and looking up into that vast kaleidoscope of a ceiling to the clear panel at the very top of the roof. I remember knowing that my mother, my twin sister, and my father were all asleep with me in that one round room, and I remember what that felt like. I do not remember that I felt poor, or hungry, or cold, but I know that I was probably all three of those things. The feeling that has stayed with me from that moment is the feeling of being home. I could not have known then about mortgages or rents, but I understood in the way small children can that this place belonged to us and not to anyone else.

I think we lived there for only a year or so. There was eventually a small fire, I think, and then maybe a failure of part of the structure, a cold winter, a period of poverty, a Vietnam war, a lack of jobs. Maybe the dome itself worked, but the world around it just didn't; maybe it was the other way around. It's hard to remember or know exactly. When we did abandon it, we didn't go far. My uncle Mike lived at the bottom of the hill in the stone house that he had built, and The Red House at the end of the road filled up with our cousins every summer, with their mothers who drove shiny station wagons and their tennis racquets and their gainfully employed fathers. Among that summerhouse circle, the dome quickly became our storied but ruined homeland. Our cousins came from Bethesda and Brooklyn, Land of Excellent Public Schools and Ballet Classes. We came from The Dome, Land of Shoelessness, Unplanned Kittens, and Head Lice. It stayed with us for a very long time. I could tell by the way my cousins used the term "The Dome" that their parents had always doubted it. And while I admit feeling awkward and different because of it, I also remember something else. I remember feeling brave.

I missed living on that mountain after we left the dome. The summerhouse wasn't our house, even though we were there as visitors a lot. We were not allowed to take food out of the cupboards or fridge, and we did not have beds there. Our cousins did, each of them with a nail in the wall where they could hang their swimsuits and hats. Their mothers, our aunts, would hang their wash on the clotheslines and tuck their children in at night, after dinners around a big, round wooden table, and then we would walk through the cold grass to my mother's car and go back to our own home, the schoolhouse, which was where we lived now, on the other side of the valley, on another mountainside. But I would remember when that hillside belonged to us. These aunts and uncles and their children had begun to spend their summers there regularly just as we had abandoned the dome, and when we visited them, they treated us like guests. Once, my aunt Jane teased me in a sweet way, telling me that there was a secret swimming pool hidden in the trees, and I realized that she didn't know that I knew this place, that I already loved this place. In the afternoons, while my cousins played and ate peanut-butter-and-jelly sandwiches and read *Mad* magazines, I would walk into the meadow between The Red House and where the dome had been and find patches of goldenrod, which my aunt Carol was allergic to, among the tall grass, and I would bend the tips into a bunch and tie them together with long pieces of grass that I would soften by wrapping them around my hands until they bent easily enough to use as a sort of string. Then I would get on my knees and use my hands and arms to push the stalks of grass and goldenrod apart at the base, flattening them down, to make a small tunnel. I would crawl inside and lie down and close my eyes. The air would be full of pollen and warm dust; the layers of old grass under me would smell like old, damp hay, and because it wasn't anyone else's home, it felt like mine.

Below the dome site, on a wide shelf that clung to the side of our mountain, which had been grazed heavily by the Combses' cows for decades until it was a rich green carpet, was my uncle Mike's house. Mike had built his house with his own hands, out of stone, when he was only eighteen years old. It stood in the spot where Donald's parents' house had once stood, and we liked to look up the mountainside from his porch and try to find the scar left on the treetops by the lightning ball. Mike had a beautiful wife, when I was young, and together they built a barn and kept horses and sheep. He lived in that house for the rest of his life, almost four more decades, with four generations of Irish setters and a string of women before and after his wife was gone, all of them beautiful and smart and tragically, desperately in love with him. No one loved Mike casually, or temporarily. There is a vein of talent that runs with a randomness through every generation in my family, a gift, a powerful collision of beauty and humor and ability, but with a dark and brutal temper that Mike had, too, and in the end he had less than nothing left. He could never leave that stone house; the place was a part of him and depended on him and defined him, so everyone, in the end, left him instead. Even us.

I like to make my teepees out of beanpoles and large pieces of netting designed to be spread over cherry trees, which are both readily available at hardware and garden supply stores. You'll need at least six 6' (1.8 m) bamboo or synthetic beanpoles, enough green or clear netting (¾" [2 cm] mesh is best) to cover the poles (one 14' x 45' [35.5 x 114 cm] piece should be more than enough); plastic zip ties long enough to generously wrap around the poles you use; and an assortment of leafy, long-stemmed plastic flowers. ● To begin, tighten a plastic zip tie around one of the beanpoles, about 8" (20 cm) from one of its ends. Tether a second pole to the first by slipping on another zip tie just below the first and wrapping it around both poles. Repeat with the remaining 4 poles. When all 6 poles have been zip-tied, stand the stack of poles upright zip-tied end up, and spread them apart at the base. Cover the teepee with the netting, leaving an opening on one side for a door. Weave the plastic flowers into the netting diagonally, overlapping flowers and their stems where possible. ● To make your teepee steadier and mobile, use sticks, shorter poles, or wooden dowels as cross-pieces to link the bottom ends of the 6 main poles to one another.

Donald's house still sits on the dirt road today, with its tin roof. At first glance it seems unusually suited to survival in that climate, compared to the ones that my family left behind, yet it may outlast them all. Wood and stone, after all, are organic materials; tin and plastic are not and cannot be digested by the land they sit on. Donald's family name and mine can be found together in the tiny graveyard at the end of the road. My grandmother's grave is marked by a simple, tasteful Gothic cross of stone. She was a woman of exacting taste and style. A few yards away lies a member of the Combs family, under a glossy granite tombstone emblazoned with an image of a gleeful man on his Ski-Doo snowmobile.

For fifteen years or so after we left the dome, we could still see it clearly from the road, its bare skeleton of big beams rising up among an increasingly overgrown meadow. Eventually the trees around it grew, and its beams were salvaged and used for something else. No one has grazed horses or cows or sheep there for more than twenty years, so even the cleared patch of meadow around it and the flat expanse where my mother's vegetable garden and my beanpole teepee were have now been completely overtaken by a young forest of birch and maple. I hiked around up there a few years ago and found nothing of the structure itself left. I wasn't even sure I was in the right spot until I found, gleaming white on the forest floor and surrounded by thick moss, the big porcelain double sink that had once stood in our kitchen. Had it not been such a surreal thing to find in the middle of the woods, and had it weighed less than fifty pounds, I would have carted it back with me, not just for the sake of nostalgia, mind you, but because it was a beautiful sink. It was the kind of sink that, if I had come across it at the 25th Street flea market in New York City, I would have paid a fortune for, found a way to drag home ten blocks, and redesigned my kitchen around. Removing it from its natural habitat, however, seemed like a sacrilege.

Mike's house is a ruin now. It suffered a fire that took its roof and several of its most important beams. The outer stone walls and giant chimney remained, but Mike wasn't young enough or strong enough anymore to rebuild it. He brought a school bus onto the property, and he and his girlfriend lived there until a few years later, when he died. The way it all looked to us, after he was gone, with its still-blackened beams partially hidden under tarps and snow, was too much for any of us to bear, and soon after the property around it, including The Red House and the dome site, was put up for sale. A man named Adam Guettel bought it, and the deal closed, ironically, on my wedding day.

My husband and I settled in New York City, because of his job and because we thought it would be exciting. We began to miss the country immediately and started looking for a weekend house in the scrappier part of the Catskill Mountains, where we knew we could afford something by, or even on, a lake, and close enough to the city to get there on a weekend. I knew, but did not say, that I was afraid of being in a small town again. On one real estate expedition we stumbled across a grand old house, hidden away in a secretive summer community where most residents were third-, even fourth-, generation owners, most of them also weekend and summer residents. It had been left for dead, untouched for decades. Its pipes had burst long ago, its furnace and copper gutters had been stolen and scrapped, and its second and third floors had been dismantled, piece by piece, by the last owner, a mentally ill and bankrupt artist.

This house and the house next door to it had been built by the same family in 1906, and the house next door, it turned out, was where a Mr. Adam Guettel spent his childhood summers. His family sold the property when he was still young, after his very young brother died there of an asthma attack. We have, it seems, by fate or coincidence or luck, traded our sad, storied histories for fresh beginnings. I sent him a note about the sink, which I hadn't been able to forget, and asked him if he would mind if I went back to collect it, and bring it back to the Catskills, and make my kitchen around it. He told me that it would make him very happy if I did just that.

I found out that I was pregnant three weeks after we closed on the house. The winter that followed was one of the coldest and snowiest in years, but we tore the place down to its bones and had it rebuilt. We watched as the house slowly started to come back to life, until we had very little energy or money left to give it, which was about the same time my daughter was born.

I did not build my house in the Catskills, and it belongs to the bank. My plastic flower teepee, however, which lives in its yard in the summertime, is totally paid for. You can feel the difference when you are inside. In the late afternoon I pick it up—which I would never be able to do with a beanpole teepee—and move it a few feet in one direction or the other, so that it sits on warm, dry grass, then I crawl inside and lie on my back. My daughter doesn't know anything, yet, about mortgages or rents, so I think I can still give her an unbroken chain of homes that feel like her own, until my house becomes hers. She is also young enough not to think that a mother who crawls inside a teepee made of plastic flowers and lies on her back with her feet poking out the door is crazy, but she will. It's OK. I once believed my parents were crazy, too, but now I know that they were brave.

HOW TO
make paper flowers

ONE SEPTEMBER, WHEN MY MOTHER was newly single and thirty and my sister and I were very small and did not yet go to school, we left Vermont and went to Mexico. We drove there in our little blue pickup truck, trailing my grandparents, who made the trip annually to San Miguel de Allende where they had a winter home. They had purchased a second house for us, large and lovely and made from pink brick, with terraces and a high wall that went all around its perimeter and from which you could see the winding cobblestone roads and the city center, with its massive, baroque Gaudí-esque cathedral and jungle-like central plaza. San Miguel had emerged in the nineteenth century as one of central Mexico's grand and rich colonial cities, full of large and elegant homes, and now it was beginning to attract Americans and Europeans and even Jack Kerouac himself, who wrote home praising the city and its fresh orange juice and agave bars where nobody noticed if you didn't have shoes and passed out on the dirt floor with your hand in your pants. It was a promise that brought a parade of bohemians and artists, and, for my mother, inappropriate suitors, streaming into the city limits.

Now, living in Manhattan, I hear a lot about how artists have been priced out of my neighborhood, and nearby SoHo and Greenwich Village. "How terrible," they say, "that the artists that made this neighborhood so vibrant cannot afford to live here anymore." I am always tempted to remind them that I, their neighbor, in fact make a living as an artist, but I know that I'm not the type of artist that they mean. I am also tempted to tell them what it was like in San Miguel in the 1970s, when the city was teeming with artists living like kings on next to nothing. I can't say for certain that the SoHo of the late 1960s that everyone seems so nostalgic for was similar because I wasn't there. But I can tell them about the parade of men who lived in rented rooms in San Miguel, about their empty canvases and quiet typewriters, their unpaid rents and their empty bottles. And I can tell them about the pained expressions that the men wore when they appeared on our doorstep, always just in time for dinner, and how they sat at our long wooden table and complained and complained and complained about being alone and invisible. If they were really alone, I remember thinking, then they would not be eating all of our cheese.

After dinner they would want to go out, and my mother would walk them to the door and say good-bye because she had two little girls to take care of and couldn't leave us to go to parties or bars. Sometimes, when we woke up, they would be there, asleep on our couches or sitting in our kitchen, waiting for someone to ask them about themselves or give them something to eat or drink. They were almost living with us, helping themselves to our food and our books and our comfortable sofas and chairs and taking up a lot of our mother's time and attention, and when they left, they never said when they were coming back.

They seemed never to add anything to what we had, and often took something of ours away with them. They spent their days at bullfights and at the Gato Negro, the agave bar that women were not allowed to go to, and sometimes they took my mother to long, lazy lunches with lots of wine and beer, for which she almost always paid, on the verandas of the big hotels, or they sat on our terrace and drank and smoked and talked about themselves, their parents, the life they'd left behind. They did everything, it seemed, except produce art.

"He is a painter. We went to RISD together," my mother said about one young, thin man who seemed to be spending most of his time looking into the cut-tin mirror in our hall, fretting over the slow growth of the beard he was attempting. "What do you paint?" I asked him one day. He threw back his head and let out an exasperated groan, then looked around to see if he had an adult audience. My mother and her girlfriend, who were sitting nearby on the floor smoking and poring through an American newspaper that one of them had found, looked up at him. "This kid wants to know," he said to them, holding back his laughter, his arm outstretched toward me, "what I *paint*." He then let out a snort, a disgusted, angry sound that made me jump. "She's just a little kid," said my mother's friend, putting out her cigarette and giving him a look that made his arms drop to his sides. The skinny man left, not because he felt bad, but because he required, as most of these men did, a constant and agreeable audience.

There was the man who would come and bend our silverware into little animal shapes. We especially liked the fork that became a giraffe with very little effort. He also tried to make a lion and a monkey and something called a manatee out of other metal utensils, but none of them worked out as well as the giraffe, which had made us jump and clap, and all of them ended up, unfinished and unusable, in the kitchen drawer. We were not tall enough to see into the drawer, but we could reach it and open it and would feel around for spoons to eat our melon with at breakfast and, inevitably, stab ourselves with the bent tines and handles that he had left, wondering whether the one, wondrous little giraffe he had wooed us with was worth the trouble. I thought it was; my sister thought it wasn't, so I took the giraffe and put him in my room, where he would be safe.

Mexico was, to children who had only known Vermont winters, a colorful paradise. On our fourth birthday, which was in November, my grandfather sent a man with two donkeys to our door. They wore tiny carved and painted wood and leather saddles and were covered in brightly colored paper flowers. They looked like toys. We thought that they were ours to keep forever, not just for a quick ride around our neighborhood, and we cried when we had to give them back. My grandfather thought that we were behaving like spoiled children and couldn't understand how we had fallen so deeply in love with something that had spent most of the afternoon trying to chew off our feet. We didn't mind that. We were, after all, the same children who had tried to make a pet out of a bitey chipmunk that was a little foamy around the mouth, even though we had seen *Old Yeller* twice. The man who owned the donkeys didn't want to leave us so unhappy, so he let us keep the paper flowers even though they were very old and beautiful and special to him, which made us stop crying so hard.

That night my mother had a birthday cake for us. We didn't know any other children in San Miguel, so our only guest was the man who had ruined our silverware. He wore a clean shirt and had washed and brushed his hair, and he carried a big bottle of beer and two little clay dishes painted with white flowers. When he saw the paper flowers, he pushed his plate aside and took one of them in both hands and begged us to let him take it apart to see how it was made. We reluctantly said yes, and made him promise to put it back together, but it was still in pieces when we went to bed. The next morning when we came back into the living room, it was sitting on the table, still deflated and broken, next to a glass of wine, and he was nowhere in sight even though we had woken up to the sound of his voice through our bedroom wall. We pushed it back together the best we could and strung it, along with the others, high over our beds. We loved the paper flowers, and when we left that house we would have taken them with us in the back of the truck, even though they would have used up half the space, but we didn't know when we left that we were not coming back.

The next winter we were back in Vermont and started the first grade. Our fifth birthday was spent not riding festooned donkeys through cobblestone streets in warm, dry air, but watching snow fall as our mother split firewood into pieces small enough to fit into our belchy stove. We opened gifts and pushed them aside and made paper flowers out of the tissue that they had been wrapped in, just like in Mexico, and wore them on our heads to dinner.

I went back to Mexico twenty years later to study art. It was the freshly squeezed orange juice, the affordable living, and maybe even the promise of inappropriate suitors that drew me there. I worked illegally as an artist's model—my Spanish was too awful to find work as a waitress or guide—and studied silver-casting and jewelry-making. I even took a class on making those big paper flowers that I had loved so much, and filled my little house with them, stringing them on the lines that were on my roof, meant for laundry. My roommate, Daniel, and I

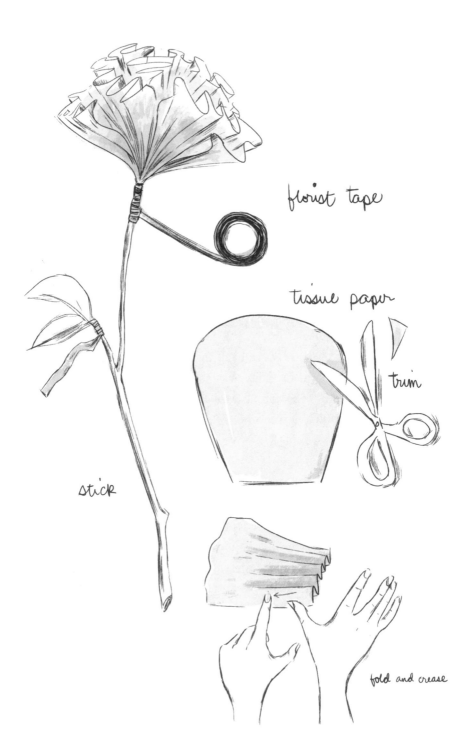

florist tape

tissue paper

trim

stick

fold and crease

threw parties and invited everyone we met that looked interesting. One thin, blond girl in an expensive-looking leather coat came to one of these dinners. She seemed incapable of a smile. She was, it turned out, an artist from New York. From *SoHo*. She seemed very serious for someone who was only twenty-one and clearly was experienced at things like parties in other countries, in strangers' houses. I was sitting next to her when she tried to light a cigarette. I told her politely that we smoked only on our roof, never inside, and pointed to the door that led to the spiral

To make paper flowers you'll need a few rolls of green floral tape; a few long sticks (2'–3' [61–91 cm] long with a diameter of about ¼"–½" [6–12 mm]); some large cone-style coffee filters; and, if you like, paint or ink to embellish your petals and green crepe paper for leaves. ● To begin, open up your coffee filters along their side and bottom seams, then cut them in half along the fold. Trim the corners on the wider top of each piece. Make small pleats with your fingers along the bottom edge, pressing the creases with your fingers. Wrap the filter around your stick, about an inch from its tip, maintaining the creases while you work. Stretch and wind your floral tape around the wrapped petal several times; leave your tape attached as you continue to add more petals. Continue to add petals, as few as three or four and as many as 40 will give you flowers of varying sizes and fullness. Wrap tape down and around your "stem" carefully, preserving its natural shape wherever possible, until you reach its bottom tip. Add leaves or other flowers to your stem, if desired. ● To make leaves (optional), cut leaf shapes from a piece of green crepe paper, and fold them in half lengthwise to make a crease. Wrap the bottom edge of your leaf around your stem and secure by wrapping your tape around it. Once you have everything attached to your stem, spread your coffee filter petals apart and trim the edges, if necessary. You can add some color by painting the petals with a brush or dipping the tips into water that has ink or paint added to it. To create an ombré effect, dampen the petals with water before brushing on paint.

staircase and our rooftop, from which, I added, you could see most of the city. She scowled and put her lighter away. "I came to Mexico because it is a lawless country," she announced, "not to be told what I can and cannot do." She wasn't looking at me directly when she said this, which almost made it worse, and then she was gone with her little pack of thin, sleek friends within ten minutes. Daniel made fun of her for the next four months. His impression was dead-on by Christmas. I would stick my head in the bathroom when he was in the shower to remind him that he was using all of our hot water, and he would shout back, "I came to Mexico because it is a lawless country!" and we would laugh at the thin little blond artist who actually thought that there was a place in the world where everyone could do exactly what they wanted, just because they were an artist.

As hard as I tried to avoid unsuitable suitors, of which there seemed to be a wide selection, I fell hard for perhaps the biggest cad in San Miguel. His name was Beso, and he was a street dog, literally, who ranked near the top of the local pack. I didn't know it when I fell for him, but he was an infamous scallywag. Beso attached himself to a different blond graduate student with a comfortable apartment every term, and for the fall/holiday term of 1993, that student was me. He was matted and flea-infested, yet tall and handsome with deep, somber eyes. Like the girls before me, I tried to take him in and make him clean and good and house-worthy, convinced that I could change him, fix him, that what we had together was different, special. But he preferred to maintain the freedom to roam, dusk to dawn, with an imposing pack of feral dogs that was known citywide.

Beso didn't live with me. He was a visitor, scratching at my heavy wooden door in the early, early morning, smelling of trash and street and a night's worth of carousing. I would always let him in, give him a little scold, and let him follow me back to bed. I would tell him he could sleep only at the foot of the bed, but when I woke up he was always next to me, his head tucked under my chin. My weakness for him, and my ancient and drafty stone house, made it impossible to push him away. He would have his breakfast with me then walk me to the studio or work, where he would wait outside my classrooms and flirt with the girls or beg for pastry at the canteen. He loved taking long naps in the protected gardens of the old hacienda that was our campus. Afterward, he would come back home with me for a good meal of chicken and rice and a small siesta, but he would always want out by dusk and be gone again until early morning. I would try to convince him to stay, to keep him with me for company in the evenings, when I had a fire going and felt especially far from home, but he would grow restless and always leave at dusk.

I also happened to be dating someone at the time, a smarmy, handsome man from New Zealand who I was pretty sure had a very serious girlfriend waiting for him at home. Malcolm was a mountain climber and a photographer, but I had never seen him do either of those things. He seemed to own a lot of cameras and ropes, but mostly they were just gathering dust in San Miguel. He claimed to be waiting for the climbing season to begin in South America, a date that depended on weather conditions. He and Beso didn't trust each other at all. "Would it be possible for him to stink more profusely?" Malcolm asked me in the middle of the night, when they were both sleeping in my bed, though neither had actually been invited to do so. This, coming from a man who had been wearing the same pair of wool socks since I met him weeks earlier. "No," I replied, "I don't think so." Beso hated him back. When I put two plates full of dinner for Malcolm and me on the coffee table in front of the fireplace one evening and went back to the kitchen for wine, I thought I heard the scraping of silverware against pottery. It didn't look like anything had been touched while I was gone—for a street dog Beso was surprisingly respectful of my food and belongings—but when Malcolm turned on the light above us and began eating, I realized that the piece of chicken on his plate had been licked thoroughly, the chili, orange, and butter glaze that I had spent two hours reducing over low heat and had carefully spooned over our plates was gone from his. Mine was clearly intact. "I think I forgot to dress your chicken, Malcolm," I said, getting up to fetch more before he realized what had happened. "It's all right," he said. "I prefer simple, whole foods anyway. Heavy sauces slow me down." I looked over at Beso, sleeping like a shaggy lion in front of the fire, and could see that he agreed.

Malcolm left San Miguel without really saying good-bye. We were walking through the market on what I thought was at least a few days before he was heading south. He bought me a tiny little raccoon carved from wood and asked me to hold it while he took my picture from twenty feet away, then he turned and walked into the crowd and was gone. Daniel was waiting for me at home, and we sat on our roof and drank beer until it was late, and I went to bed not knowing who would be scratching on my door in the morning. I woke up at dawn to the sound of Beso pushing his nose into my mail flap. I opened the door for him, and he followed me back to bed. When I finally got up for coffee with Daniel, I stepped on a pile of tiny splinters of wood; the little wooden raccoon that Malcolm had given me had been chewed into bits and left in a small heap. Beso looked very pleased with himself. I gave him the half chicken in the fridge and put some ice cubes in his water bowl, his favorites.

On the day I left the city for good, Beso stuck to me like never before. I think he knew all the signs from all the girls before me and thought maybe one of us would take him back with us to wherever it was that we had come from. But I was going to be traveling for many more months and then returning to a cabin and a job in a California state park where dogs were not allowed, so I could not take him with me. I missed him painfully for more than a year, feeling as though I had let him down, broken his heart.

A few months after I returned to California, I got a letter from Malcolm, who had finally made it back to San Miguel after a year of climbing in Patagonia. The first two pages were minute accounts of his climbing expeditions, full of a language I didn't understand, and the next-to-the-last paragraph was about Beso. He was, according to this report, living like a king in the arms of a pretty pottery graduate student named Lucia, whom we had both known. She had just taken a job as a teacher at the Belles Artes, and so would never be leaving the city, at least not in Beso's lifetime. Then there were a few sentences about why it had been too hard to say good-bye to me, and how he had hoped I would still be there when he came back through but could not have known how long that would be. He was going back to New Zealand and to his girlfriend, whom he had grown close to through letters during his absence and harrowing, valiant climbing expeditions, and they would likely be married by Christmas.

I sat for a long time with this letter in my hands, feeling freshly jealous and thinking of our time together and wondering whether Beso thought of me often, or at all. The only thing I could find consolation in was knowing that Lucia was a vegetarian.

Just after I was married (to an appropriate suitor) and had moved to New York City, I stumbled across Lobo on the website of an organization called Stray from the Heart, which places homeless dogs in loving homes. Many of their dogs come from Quito, Ecuador, where a veterinarian named Linda literally picks up animals off the streets, administers necessary care (in Lobo's case, tending to a badly broken hip), and finds them new homes in the United States. A few months later, I stood in the baggage area of LaGuardia airport. Fifteen years after I had said good-bye to Beso at the San Miguel bus station, I was saying hello to Lobo, who was looking up at me from his dark crate with an expression similar to the one that Beso had worn the day I had left him. It was a face formed by decades of natural selection, through countless generations, an expression that conveyed an intelligence and a charm that could both recognize the source of a warm meal and a bed and find a way, instantly, to win her heart.

HOW TO
make coffee logs
to start a fire

WHEN WE RETURNED FROM Mexico, my mother, sister, and I moved into the one-room schoolhouse on West Hill. Our father was living in Virginia, near his parents, and we would see him only sporadically for the next few years. My grandfather had purchased the schoolhouse property from a friend, a Mr. Tyler, who had never returned to it after buying it as a romantic notion for his wife, who had proclaimed it to include the prettiest spot in all of Vermont. It sat on the twenty acres that bordered West Hill Brook on one side and a gravel road on the other. We could walk or run through the woods on a path that had been made by schoolchildren a century before us to the covered bridge that sat over a clear, deep pool at the bottom of a steep waterfall. It was surrounded by rock ledges that were perfect for jumping from. In the summer the schoolhouse and the land around it were a paradise, but in the winter it was all we could do to stay warm and fed.

The house had come with a resident tomcat that we loved instantly. His name was Teddy, and he was such a wet-black color that even when you were very close to him, it was difficult to make out the shape of his chin or where his legs began. Usually it was just his eyes that you could see, and they were used to convey little else than a mixture of wisdom and intense annoyance. He had already been inhabiting the schoolhouse when we moved into it, so no one knew for sure how old he was. Now, when I think of him living with us—a young, beautiful, broke single mother and two little girls on top of a cold mountain—and dropping plump mice, still warm and shaggy in their winter coats, on our pillows in the early morning, I believe it was because he knew far better than we did how close we three toed the line of survival.

Teddy's strategy for getting through a Vermont winter was similar to our mother's: sleep through as much of it as possible. In the coldest months he would curl up for hours and hours under the potbelly woodstove that was our main source of heat, sometimes for so long that his whiskers would begin to twist up at the tips and his thick black fur crackled when you touched it. My sister and I would dry off in front of the stove after our bedtime baths while he watched us suspiciously from underneath, peering out between the chrome claw feet. We would wait until his eyes had closed, yank him out by his thick tail, and run as fast as we could, clutching him in our arms, trying to get him into our bed while he was still hot. Then we would stuff him under the covers and scramble around, holding the blankets down in every direction. The point was not to convince him to stay; it was just to keep him under there long enough to warm things up. He would eventually tear his way free, throwing disgusted glances over his shoulder as he marched back to his stove. We would wake up hours later, with the stove gone out and the house filled with that dusty, cold blue morning light, to find him stretched out with stiff legs against our backs, pushing us slowly off our mattress, stealing back his heat.

My mother's bed was very close to the stove and also to the door that led to the small addition that had been built onto the back of the house where my sister and I slept. My mother had put up wallpaper in our room that had pictures of animals—lambs and kid goats and bunnies—dancing together in a flowery meadow. In the beginning she had matched up the design perfectly, but then as she worked toward the other end of the wall, she must have decided that it wasn't worth the effort because she stopped trying. My bed was against a wall where the images on the wallpaper didn't match up perfectly, and I would lie on my side and run my fingers over the edges of the paper where they overlapped, trying to push the halves of the images together in my mind. We slept under heavy Mexican blankets and wore thick, footed pajamas but would still wake up, uncomfortable from the cold, and need to crawl into each other's beds. When

I crept into my sister's bed, she would let me sleep next to the wall, where I could press my fingers against the same images where they matched up exactly, and next to her warmth the cold muscles in my legs and arms would warm and relax, and I would fall asleep. If I looked through the doorway as I walked from one bed to the other, I could see Teddy tucked into the folds of the Mexican blankets on my mother's bed, where he had been since his stove had gone out.

My mother was very good at starting fires and at keeping them going. When she brought an armload of firewood into the house and dropped it onto the wood floor next to the stove, there would be three or four medium-size logs and one or maybe two very large ones. Those were the ones that would keep burning—with luck, and if the dampers were set properly—through the night, and theirs would be the embers that would make a crackling morning fire quick work. We had no woodshed, so the logs would be coated with snow and chunks of ice and would need to be set on their ends leaning against the chrome skirt around the base of the stove to dry. If the stove went out in the middle of the night, we would wake up cold, and we could find our mother in her flannel nightgown, her bare hands reaching through the door of the stove, a box of strike-anywhere matches on the floor next to her. We would climb into her bed and pull her blankets over us and watch her work, and sometimes Teddy would watch with us. She sometimes had her boots on, under her nightgown, which meant that she either had had to go out for more wood or felt that it might be necessary to give the stove a swift kick.

There were two mountains visible from a high spot on our road. They were across the valley, round and smooth like most of the Green Mountains, which are older and more weather-worn than the tall and spiny mountains in the west. One of the ridgelines, the larger and higher of the two, makes a slow S-curve before dropping into the valley. The other is a soft lump tucked into one of these curves, so close in one place that the valley between them rises a bit. Almost every time we drove past the spot where they became visible for a moment, we would point and shout out that those mountains looked just like my mother and Teddy asleep together, under thick blankets. When there was snow on the mountains, they looked especially peaceful, as though they would be asleep for months, the top of my mother's head barely visible beneath stiff, white wool blankets.

I have a photograph on my wall now, a tiny black-and-white picture of our schoolhouse. The house itself is barely visible; just the peaked roofline and the top of our door can be seen past a massive pile of firewood. It was delivered this way, dumped from the back of a truck right in front of our door, not stacked. That would have cost us extra. The wood in the photo is covered in a fresh foot of snow. It is, to my eye, a photograph of a family who was caught unprepared for winter. They did not get their wood delivered on time or had not stacked it up and protected it with a tarp against the house, under the eaves. They must have spent more than one miserable day pulling apart a frozen pile of wood with wool mittens, though I don't remember that. My mother likely did that alone while my sister and I were inside, watching whatever was on the one channel we got on our tiny black-and-white television or, more likely, harassing Teddy. I see this photo and I remember the way that some of the people in town looked at my mother, as though she must be crazy to be living the way she was, with two little girls on a mountain road in an uninsulated house with no electric heat. I see this photo, taken from our road and from the perspective our neighbors must have had as they drove past our house, and I imagine them shaking their heads in judgment as they went by.

Some winters our wood would arrive unsplit. It would appear as short logs, trees cut into lengths that would fit into our stove, and my mother would borrow or rent a wood splitter to cut it into sections. When the wood splitter was in the yard, my sister and I were not allowed to go outside. It was a noisy thing, louder than a mower or a car, and spit out a smelly, oily smoke that would cling to my mother's hair for days afterward. She was unimaginably strong, my mother. Tall and very thin, with long, thick red hair that was always down, and always loose. She was very beautiful. By my math she was thirty-three, maybe thirty-four, when the photo of the woodpile under the snow was taken.

On these fall mornings she dressed in the ragg-wool sweaters and thermal undershirts that my grandmother bought her every year for Christmas, with jeans. She had a thick wool fisherman's hat that she would pull over her head, pushing her hair over her ears underneath it to keep it out of her way. She would make herself coffee in a percolator, dumping the dried coffee grounds from the morning before into the stove before making a fresh pot. They would make the fire very hot for just a moment, a bright orange glow would rise up, and we would say that the stove and our mother loved coffee in the morning equally.

When she was running the splitter, lifting logs that must have weighed fifty pounds onto its belt and pushing them into a sharp, rotating saw blade, she would get very hot and take off her sweater and then her hat, and then even her gloves, and then we would see her through the window, sleeves pushed past her elbows, lifting and pushing, her breath like clouds, until the engine would cut out because she was tired or because she had run out of fuel, and then she would sit on an unsplit log and have a cigarette, and stretch her back like a cat, and then the other way, so that she would be looking up at the gray sky, with smoke coming out of her mouth and her eyes closed. Then she would come inside and make us dinner, usually spaghetti, and we would all crawl into her bed together and watch television. Teddy would come out from under the stove, walk over us with heavy, quick steps, and curl up next to her head, and she would scratch him under the chin and pet him, and he would raise his chin and close his eyes, and he would purr. She had boyfriends in those days, but they were mostly not around when we were awake, and they were never there to help her with things like firewood, though they might have been if she had asked. The only man in her life, as far as we could see, who paid attention to whether the house was warm enough, was Teddy.

I had forgotten, until recently, what depending on wood heat means. When Hurricane Sandy inched toward my city, I got an e-mail from my mother, who still lives in Vermont. She has a little house in town now and doesn't live in the school-house anymore. She even has oil heat, because after decades of depending on wood heat for survival, after years of battling old woodstoves and undependable weather patterns and inhaling dust and smoke, she decided that she had dedicated enough hours of her life to trying to stay warm and put down her ax for good. She also has cable television, which has replaced the potbelly woodstove as the thing that she moves her chair toward and that makes her angry and that sometimes gets a swift kick in its side. She watched closely the morning of October 28, 2012, and could see that storm coming and went upstairs to her computer and typed out the following message to me: "That Sandy looks mean. Get the fuck out of there. Come here if you want."

We were already leaving the city when I got her message. I had packed a week's worth of food and water, our warmest clothing and boots, our battery-powered radio and lanterns, shelf-stabilized milk, my one-year-old daughter, my dog, and my husband into our car, a four-thousand-pound, twenty-year-old Land Cruiser, and was checking traffic patterns. There were moments, over the course of that morning, when I felt supremely, almost irrationally, confident, even as I watched people on the streets below through my bedroom window, carrying on with their day as though there was no reason to flee or even carry a raincoat. It was sunny and bright, and according to the radio there was no traffic on the FDR, even though an evacuation of Lower Manhattan had been called during a much less severe storm the year prior. But there were also moments when I wondered if I was overreacting. I remembered a dinner party, about a year after I had moved to New York City. We were with some friends of my husband's from business school, most of whom had grown up in or near the city. I had embarrassed myself by launching into a speech—after two drinks on an empty stomach—about how important it was for each of us to have an escape plan were there ever to be a catastrophe, natural or otherwise, stressing that the evacuation routes from the city were not adequate. This would have been a perfectly normal thing to say in my former social circles, in northern California and rural Vermont, where paranoia and a distrust of public services in the face of natural disasters were standard.

But here it was followed by a still silence, a circle of faces with raised brows and wry smiles. Tricia Spielman reached across the table and put her hand on top of mine. "Don't worry, Heather, we keep a car uptown." And then she raised her other hand to her ear with her pinky and index fingers extended, to indicate a phone, and tilted her head, saying, "If anything happens, just call me. We'll come get you."

We drove two hours to our house in the Catskills, where we also expected to lose power but knew, or hoped, that we would be able to stay warm with wood fires, something I had not done for a decade, and even then it hadn't been in a deadly cold.

We lost power the following evening, even earlier than expected. We watched two trees, each sixty or seventy feet tall, land on our power lines, causing them to snap in half. TC and I pulled Bee's crib into our bedroom, where we sat awake as she slept, with the dog between us, listening to massive pines and firs hitting the ground as the winds touched down. We heard the cable that connected us to the grid snap away from the house and watched it fly toward its other end, still connected to a now-downed pole, which hung eerily over our driveway. We made wood fires in our smoky fireplaces and stuffed cracks in windows and doors, but our house was too big to heat with just fireplaces. Plus, the ultra-sensitive smoke alarms wouldn't stop going off, waking us and Bee every hour and giving us constant headaches. Our house was failing us and clearly needed power to operate. We made the decision to move to a smaller house nearby, owned by close friends. They were in New Jersey, also without power, but were able to get us a message telling us that it was what they wanted us to do, knowing that we would be able to keep it warm with its one central woodstove. We packed everything we could and moved on foot—our car was trapped by fallen trees—through the stormy woods and set up home for the next five days in their efficient little house.

TC has never depended on wood heat the way I have. He can start a fire and keep it going, but he lacks the inner anxiety alarm that reminds him to maintain it. I had never been dependent on wood heat as a mother before, and I realized quickly that it creates a whole new set of alarms, anxiety, and fear. Bee was dressed in her warmest clothing. We didn't have running water to bathe her, but I could fill a bucket in the stream or lake and warm it on the gas stove. I fed her and TC and the dog bacon and bread with butter, what TC began to refer to as my "anxious Eskimo diet." I made sure we were all drinking enough water, and I watched the stove without blinking. What I could not manage to do was build a fire that would keep burning through the entire night, so I slept with an eye open, and got up in the dark in the wee hours, and rebuilt it. My baby and husband kept sleeping. It would stay warm upstairs long after the fire had gone out below, but my dog would join me in the cold, sitting next to me as I bent over in front of the stove as it lit up and filled the room with a warm, faded light.

I could not go back to sleep, so the dog and I would make coffee with a percolator, dumping the grounds from the previous morning into the woodstove, which would swallow them with a hot belch, and sit together and make a plan to get through the day, silently calculating the amount of water, of milk for the baby, of firewood, that we would need. Eventually, my family would wake up and join us, and while we were happy to be safe and warm together, I was getting tired. The fact that my mother had done this, with two tiny children and a tomcat instead of a husband, for four years, seemed impossible. In the months after Sandy, I became preoccupied with discovering a way to heat my house with something other than wood. A friend's husband, intrigued by my efforts, got involved. By Christmas, I had a plan.

To make a coffee log fire starter, preheat oven to 260°F (120°C). Spread 2½ cups (570 g) spent coffee grounds (donated by a local coffee shop) in a large baking dish, and place on the lower rack of the oven. Place ¾ cup (180 ml) molasses and 1¼ cups (280 g) wax pieces (break up 3–4 emergency candles or a block of craft wax) in a 9" x 5" (23 x 12 cm) loaf pan, and place in the oven next to the coffee grounds. Cook for 20 minutes, or until grounds are completely dry. Remove both pans from the oven and add the grounds to the melted wax and molasses mixture ½ cup (115 g) at a time, until all of the grounds are shiny and dark with wax and molasses; if the grounds sizzle as you add them, they are still damp and need to dry out a bit longer. To flatten the mixture, lay a piece of foil or plastic wrap across the top and press on the surface with your hands until it's compacted and flat in the loaf pan. Allow to cool and harden for a few hours (or less if you put it outside in the cold). Pry the "log" loose with a butter knife and remove from pan. If desired, wrap the log in paper, which looks pretty and will help you to light it later. For a lovely gift, wrap a few logs in paper and tie them together with a flammable paper ribbon.

HOW TO
make a bonfire

BEGINNING IN THE EARLY 1970s, my aunt Jane spent every summer with her three children at The Red House, taking responsibility for opening it every June and closing it down every September, and always managing to dismiss its substantial shortcomings in much the same way she managed to ignore those of the family that she had married into. My aunt Carol came, too, from Brooklyn, with her two boys in tow, but she loved it less and was burdened with allergies and a fear of the dogs and horses that my uncle Mike kept at his nearby farm. Carol seemed to be there because she had to be, to escape the city and a house with no air-conditioning, not because she really wanted to be.

The house was already old and crooked by the time my grandfather owned it. The barn that had stood next to it for three-quarters of a century was finally torn down when I was still in grade school because it had become a haven for wasp nests and unsafe clubhouses. Without anyone living and cooking in it and keeping the lawn short, the house would have been swallowed up by the ground it sat on and the woods around it in less than a decade. But, for twenty-five years, The Red House had Jane to come every spring and sweep it out, and to put clean sheets on its terrible old, stained mattresses and pots of geraniums in front of its decomposing foundation, and to cook big aluminum pots full of corn on the cob and spaghetti on its cheap electric stove, and to convince us, each in our own way, that it was a house and a place worth loving, that even its most hazardous issues were nothing more than charming life-in-the-country quirks.

The Red House was a simple farmhouse with a stone foundation and a basement so creepy that you had to speed up your steps when you walked past the door that led there, with its weak little latch that always looked as though something had been pushing against it from the other side. Its attic housed a healthy bat population, its foundation seemed to be made mostly of mice, and its attached woodshed appeared to be at least the weekend home to a family of overweight, slow-moving porcupines who had eaten all of the firewood long ago and had started to chew on the walls and floors. If you complained about these things to Jane, she would turn up her little radio, which was always tuned to the BBC station out of Montreal. When the radio wasn't on, Jane would hum to herself, short little classical tunes. If you went to her room, the door to which was always open, and complained that it was too hot at night and that you could not fall asleep, she would say, "There is a wonderful, cool breeze coming through my window just now, so if you run back to your bed, you'll be there in time to feel it come through your room and out your window." You would believe her and run back to bed, put at ease, and then you would fall asleep waiting for that breeze, which you were never quite sure if you had felt or not.

The bugs would get so bad in June and early July that you would sometimes need to run from the car to the front door, and the clover that choked out the grass in the acres of lawn around the house and the thickets of berry bushes at its edges drew more bees and wasps and hornets than you could easily avoid. Jane kept a bowl of baking soda and water on the kitchen table, which quickly drew out the sting of stepping on a bee with your bare foot, and she hung awful, ugly flypapers in the kitchen to catch the more obnoxious blackflies that found their way in. Jane loved to hike and pick berries in the woods around The Red House, where the bugs would be especially hungry and thick, so she fashioned herself a new hat from an old Chinese straw hat and some beekeeper's netting. She would often be wearing this hat, along with a pale blue oxford shirt, her tennis shorts, a red bandana tied over her hair, and worn tennis shoes, when we pulled up onto the lawn. She would greet us with a wave, one hand on a hip, the other high above her head, with just her fingertips wiggling, all on tiptoe, and then skip off again. My mother would shake her head and mutter, "What is she on?"

The house's steep staircase was deadly, and each of us remembers falling down it at least once. Its handrail was only helpful for the first half of the descent, because it was actually a broomstick that wasn't quite long enough to cover the span of stairs, and because the person who had attached it to the wall was clever enough to have threaded a wooden spool onto the nail between the stick and the wall at one end, but had not done so at the other, so if you used it without looking, your fingers would get stuck before you reached the bottom of the stairs, which would be confusing—not a helpful state of mind to be in when you are two-thirds of your way down a very steep and crooked staircase. We all learned to walk down sideways, hopping from foot to foot, ignoring and hating the rail, but we rarely remembered to warn guests, who were routinely spit out at the bottom of the staircase with a crash, betrayed looks on their faces. Jane would come down the stairs with a quiet little series of hops, as though timed to music, her fingertips trailing along the top of the broomstick but never wrapped around it, and land delicately in the hall. I watched her do it once, from above, to see if I could copy it. I was terrified of the stairs, having crashed down them regularly since I was a baby. I noticed for the first time that she was smaller than most of the adults in our family, which was full of tall people, and more suited to a house like this, with its low doorways and ceilings.

My sister and I looked forward to those weeks when Jane and her children were at The Red House, with their spaghetti dinners and clean sheets. Our cousins' world seemed a stable, pretty place where there was always food in the cupboards and gas in the car, and since those were the things that we wished for, we also wished that we were a part of that world.

When Jane talked about her own childhood, it was with what seemed to be a happy nostalgia. She would tell us about the car her father had, with its bumper seat in the back, and about being allowed to ride in it on family outings. When the very first J.Crew catalog appeared on the kitchen table at The Red House, she pointed to the group of preppy youngsters around an evening bonfire on a New England beach on its cover and announced with a wistful drama and a hand clap, "*That*, children, that was me, those were my summer evenings, and oh, how I want to have a *bonfire!*" And so bonfire we did. We sat high on the top of the mountain at the end of every summer, under a thick ocean of stars with crickets all around us, with blankets crushing the tall grasses and marshmallows on sticks and songs sung in rounds. Below us, The Red House was lit from within like a lantern, warm light spilling out of its front door and windows onto the grass around it, looking like the perfect summerhouse on the perfect summer evening, just as Jane saw it, I'm sure. I loved bonfires because the light that came from them lit only the faces closest to the fire, and I could disappear slightly from sight, crawling off the blankets and into the tall grass, where I could see my family from a distance, where they looked more perfect than they were, almost like the people on the cover of the J.Crew catalog. I was certain that I did not belong, that my sister and I and our mother were not the sort of family that were found sitting around bonfires on the covers of magazines, but then I would look up at the stars, and as soon as I would begin to try to grasp the incomprehensible scale of what I was seeing, I would feel my own self and my worries grow smaller and smaller, until they were nearly gone.

Jane would often be carting all of us—her three children plus my sister and me and our two other cousins, all seven of us within just three or four years of each other—in her big Malibu station wagon, coming and going from swimming or town, and she would always be trying to organize us into a singing troupe. She would go after the most willing of us first, her youngest daughter, Rachel, and my sister and me, getting us to join her in a verse of "Row, Row, Row Your Boat." Then finally Martha would be coerced into a verse, sitting always in the front passenger seat, and then just when we all thought we were singing the final verse, Jane would cheerfully command, "Now in a round!" and point to one of us. Martha would be beside herself with embarrassment and yell at her to stop. We would see her blond head fall back and hear her shout, "Mom, *nooo!*" and then Jane would say, "Oh, Martha, you are no fun at all. Why won't you let your mother sing?" And then she would start all over again. My sister and I loved it. Our mother was a far more distracted chauffeur, needing all of her focus to speed and smoke simultaneously, always with the gas tank needle bouncing up and down against the red E line, and we were usually too busy hanging on to something, readying ourselves for the next curve in the road, to care. Jane referred to being in a car with my mother, behind her back, as Mr. Toad's Wild Ride, while my mother compared being in a car with Jane, behind her back, to being "trapped in a fucking padded wagon with a fucking Trapp Family lunatic." They were surprisingly close. Jane was able to love my mother for the same reasons that she was able to love all of us, and the house, because she refused to acknowledge the things about us that were broken or unsafe or beyond fixing. My mother would complain to Jane about the way she was treated by her other family members and by my father, and Jane would say things like, "Oh, Tess, when will you just bury the hatchet?" or "Well, yes, Tess, it's difficult to be the only sister, isn't it?" and listen. Jane never complained about her own life, or other people, at least not in front of me.

Jane and my mother would sit for hours on the deck that hung off the back of The Red House while we played in the meadow and lawn around it. On one such day, Martha and I pulled apart a rotted picnic table and surveyed the pieces. We wanted to make it into a raft and to take it fishing. We approached our mothers from the lawn for permission, shouting up at their perch on the porch, where they sat smoking and drinking wine. We and the raft, when we were finished building it, would also be needing a ride to Belvedere Bog, we explained, which was only four miles away, where we planned to spend the night so that we could be up early, which was when we understood fish to be hungry. We watched them whisper back and forth for a moment and then Jane gave us their answer. "All right, but on one condition. You must disguise yourselves to look like little old men, so that the actual fishermen don't try to make off with you." We agreed and spent an hour in the bathroom, in a serious mood as though our lives and chastity depended on it, brushing mascara onto our upper lips. It was a thrilling thing, as a child, to feel as though your own small fantasy was being encouraged by a mother, your own or someone else's.

Jane also allowed her children to ride on the back bumper of my mother's car when we were driving on the dirt roads, which was not at all safe, and allowed them to go flying with us when Tommy Phillipson, a dashing family friend (and part-time drug smuggler, it turned out), came to town with his little plane. Sometimes he let my mother or my uncle Mike take control, with all of us in the backseat, at which point I would usually throw up. We knew that many of these things were not safe, but my mother and Jane both seemed to want them for us, because they were also adventures. They both also happily ignored the fact that we went, literally, all summer without showering, and had head lice, all of us, for most of the 1980s. "Just like when we were at school!" Jane would say to my mother, who had spent her childhood in boarding schools, with nobody to tell her to take a shower or change her clothes. But Jane never said where she had gone to school.

In all of those summers, there was just one moment when I think that, just for a moment, I saw something else through a tiny crack. Jane and my mother and I had been in the kitch-en at The Red House; I was perhaps eight or nine years old.

My mother was dating a man who lived an hour or so away, a younger man I didn't know very well, whose home I had never been to. My mother and Jane had been drinking wine and smoking cigarettes all afternoon, and my mother had just announced that she would be driving, with my sister and me, to see this man. We might be spending the night there, but there was no plan apart from getting into the car in the clothes on our backs, with only possibly enough gas to make it home, with our mother, who seemed a little drunk. I told her that I didn't want to go, that I wanted to go home, or stay at The Red House. "Tough shit," she said, and pushed open the screen door with her shoulder as she lit a cigarette. "I'm having a smoke and then we are leaving."

I ran into the bathroom and sat on the side of the tub, trying to hold back tears, my stomach and my chest pounding and aching. Jane opened the door and quietly sat next to me, her hand on my back. At first she said what she always said, trying to get me to smile, but I was past the point of needing just a cheerful chin-up. What I needed, at that moment, was for someone, just once, to tell me that I was right, that even though I was a child, I was right, that this thing that felt so unfair was, indeed, unfair, that what was happening to me—the mother who was barely holding on, drinking more and more, dragging me along on her poorly planned adventures—wasn't OK. And Jane, for the first and only time in my life, did that. She pulled me up onto her lap and held me as tightly as she could and told me that she loved me, and then, over and over again, her voice cracking, she said just one thing. "I know," she said. "I know, I know, I know."

When I reached the age when I started to question anything and everything about my family and my place in it and did not want to take responsibility for my life, when I felt that I was still at a deficit for not being treated or taught or loved appropriately, and therefore was owed something, like an apology (or someone paying my rent for me; either would do), I pointed the blame at the members of my family who had seemed so content to ignore my circumstances, including Jane. Her constant state of happy delusion, I had decided, represented my mother's family's unwillingness to help us, me and my sister and my mother, when we were so clearly without so much and they seemed to have so much of everything, and so little to worry about. Why did they not worry about us?

It was during this same span of years that I pulled away from my mother and her family, and while I didn't know it at the time, my mother turned to Jane, who protected her and supported her with her unending optimism. For a short time my mother even lived near Jane in Virginia, and turned to her for emotional and financial support more than once. I was as far away as I could be by then, in California, but called Jane at some point to ask her if she knew where my mother was and how she was doing. I hadn't spoken to my mother for a long time, and I wanted very much to have a real conversation about her situation, her life, her well-being, and, I think, I probably wanted sympathy, for who and what my mother was, for what I did not have. I asked Jane, knowing that the truth was horrible. There was a silence, and for an instant I thought I would see it again, after all these years, that crack through which I would see that Jane saw us all for what we were, that we would now talk about what could be done for my mother, but then I heard her take a long inhale and then, with a chilling cheerfulness, she said, "The thing about your mother, Tupy"—she was calling me by my childhood nickname, as if to remind me that we were still safely in the land of illusion—"is that she always lands on her feet."

Jane and I spoke again the summer before I turned twenty-eight. I was still angry, still bitter, but also becoming self-sufficient, finally. I had started my own business and was, at least from a distant perspective, a functioning, successful young adult. Jane and I and her husband, my uncle, were alone together at The Red House. She seemed tired to me, and while the house felt as though she was caring for it and loving it more than ever, her energy and optimism seemed to be waning. Her children were all away, their own lives no longer allowing for long summers in Vermont. Over morning coffee she looked up at me, and with a smile and that warbling, dramatic voice coming back for just that instant, and with a brief lift of her arm, she said, "I just hate your mother for the fact that she did absolutely everything wrong, and yet you turned out perfectly!" It was meant to be funny, and actually, it was. It was also meant as a blessing, a happy proclamation, and while we both knew it wasn't totally true, it struck me that I had a better shot at making it true if someone already believed that it was. A few fleeting years later, Jane was diagnosed with cancer. Everyone seemed optimistic at first, but she died the following summer, just a few days before she had planned what I think she believed would be her last summer in Vermont.

Without Jane to defend it, discussions about The Red House seemed suddenly to be about what was wrong with it. It was falling apart, unsafe, too far away. In the span of two years, Jane was gone, and both of my grandparents, and then the house was put up for sale by my mother and uncles, who now owned it. It was something that most of my generation didn't want to have happen, but for Martha and Rachel it was especially sad, because the house had been Jane's place, and because we had scattered her ashes there. And then Martha was married, and then she was pregnant, and then one spring weekend we were all in her house—Rachel, Martha, my aunt Carol, and me—to attend her baby shower, which was being thrown by a group of Jane's closest and oldest friends at a stately suburban home. I knew that Martha was appreciative but also dreading this. I didn't think anybody at the party knew me other than my cousins and aunt, but I was wrong. A slight woman, about Jane's age, came up to me and introduced herself. "You are Tupy, aren't you? One of the twins?" I nodded. "Jane told me so much about you. We walked together, you see, for exercise, nearly every week. I have been hearing about you and your sister and your mother for so many years. It's remarkable to meet you." She was studying my face now, with wide eyes, as though she wasn't sure she could trust me. I wondered for just an instant what Jane could have been telling her, how she had managed to include us in her glowing reports of The Red House. "She was always so concerned about you both, she would worry so much, and tell me about everything that was happening to both of you. She spent so much time worrying, but what could be done?" I was too stunned to respond. It was true, I saw now. What *could* have been done? Other than loving us, other than choosing to see what we had instead of what we didn't have, other than forcing us to sing out loud and marching us up grassy hillsides to sit under the stars, other than, just once, putting her arms around us and telling us that she understood, what else could she have done?

When Jane was gone and her spell was finally broken, it became clear that her life was more ordinary, and far less perfect than what we had thought. She had never been one to talk about the negative, to waste time worrying over the unchangeable past, to dwell on the bitter or the unfair. Because of this we had thought that her life was perfect and bright, without sadness or pain, but of course that isn't true of anyone's life. And I realized that she had told me everything, she told me her secret that afternoon in The Red House, when she held me more tightly than my own mother ever had and said those two words over and over again: "I know, I know, I know."

Most importantly, Jane's happiness, and her love for her children, and her love for The Red House, and the gift that she gave my family in the form of that place through her eyes and those summers together had been very real and more profound than we could have understood when we were young. Jane's childhood had probably not even included bonfires, but because of her, mine did.

I think of Jane every time a J.Crew catalog arrives in my mailbox, which seems like every other week. There are fewer bonfires on the cover now, but just as many fresh-faced, optimistic young people who seem to be living perfect lives draped in plaid and glee. I don't resent them the way I did as a kid or look at them and wish that I had what they had. I know now that it's possible to make a bonfire at the top of a dark mountain, or to choose to live your life as a series of beautiful moments, born out of your own imagination rather than through inheritance, or legacy, or status. I know that happy moments make a happy family, and that it's not the other way around. I imagine that those catalog-cover faces are only happy in that moment, that when they get home from Aspen or Montauk or Stowe they will learn that their parents are divorcing, that they are moving far away, that their father has been in love with someone other than their mother for twenty years, that someone they love is sick and will not be getting better. But it doesn't mean they can't have a bonfire, or sing a camp song in a round, or live in some way, in a small moment, in the faint flickering light of a fire that hides more than it reveals, as though nothing in the world deserves worry.

HOW TO
catch a frog

I DON'T THINK I EVER ACTUALLY SAW THE face of the man who drove the gray Peugeot with the Quebec license plates down our dirt road on summer Monday mornings. The only time I saw his car in town, pulling up to the Village Store's gas pump, I hid from him because in my mind we were sworn enemies, though now I'm not sure he even knew that I existed. I was seven, almost eight.

I also don't know how we knew that the man in the gray Peugeot owned a French restaurant in Montreal, the kind that served frog legs. Someone told my mother and she told us, but we could tell that she thought that he was not worth knowing. The Peugeot only appeared in the summer and the early fall, and then the snow would fall heavily, as it always did in those days, and the wagon road that led up to the old farmhouse that he rented would never be plowed, and it was as though he had never been there at all.

The first time I saw the Peugeot stopped on our road, I thought it was stalled. I had woken up and noticed that our cat had not come home for two nights in a row, and was walking along the edge of the road, pushing my bike, looking into the tall weeds, hoping that I wouldn't find her there. The Peugeot looked like the kind of car that broke down a lot. Up close you could see little spots of rust along its bottom edge. Its tires looked smooth and small. It was stopped right in the middle of the road, as though the man could not have imagined anyone else needing to go anywhere. He was lucky my mother was still in bed; she drove fast and surely would have called him an a-hole and might have even run into him. The man was standing over the car's low, curvy hood, on which was balanced a tin bucket, the kind used for collecting sap from a maple tree. His shoes were shiny and flat and had square toes that stuck up in the front, so much so that I could see them doing so from the back, and his pants were tight and creased and an ugly brown. His body bulged out above his belt, and his arms looked skinny and long as he dug around in the tin bucket with quick, careful movements. His face was hidden from me.

Next to him stood Clive and Ronnie Rogers, still dressed in their barn clothes. They weren't exactly brothers but a nephew and uncle who were only a few years apart, and inseparable. Their family was a prolific lot with a confusing structure that lived in a group of houses and trailers clustered around a small cow barn at the bottom of a wet gulch about a mile from our house. The gulch always smelled of the cows that grazed its sloped perimeter, leaving thin green paths through the trees and chewing away anything that resembled grass, exposing rocky outcroppings covered with a beautiful mossy carpet that would have been perfect for wandering along if it didn't smell so sour. There were always lots of cars in their driveways, clustered together and looking related, all vaguely American, bland in color, all of them afflicted with varying amounts of the same rash-like rust.

Clive and Ronnie were just a few years older than my twin sister and me and had a sister—and/or cousin—who was just a year younger, but we never, ever considered her a potential playmate except for the one time we heard Clive bragging that they had caught a baby raccoon and were keeping it as a pet, but by the time we got there it had caused such destruction that it had been returned to the woods. I remember Clive's sad, plain little sister standing in her doorway explaining to me why raccoons did not make good pets. "They sleep during the day, and at night they rob you and chew on you." My sister and I were horrified by her callousness and spent the better part of that day walking through the marshy woods around the gulch looking for the baby raccoon. Nothing small could survive for very long without a mother here, even in the summer. We filled our pockets with cat food and made small piles of it on downed trees and on wide maple leaves, set like plates, wondering at the odds of her having been found by her mother. We decided that if we found her, we would take her home and let her chew on anything she liked. There wasn't a single item or surface in our home that required protection from chewing or scratching or dirt, and we certainly didn't have anything worth robbing. We lived without much separation between indoors and out, the presence of wildlife not being an exception, unless it was very cold, and then it was not us that the doors and windows were meant to keep in but the precious heat that we struggled to trap between our uninsulated walls.

The boys looked up at the man as though they were waiting for something. After a moment of what seemed like tense discourse, they all took a step back from the bucket, and the man reached into his pocket and pulled out his wallet, opened it, and gave each boy what looked like a dollar bill. Then he put the bucket into the trunk of his car and drove away, giving them a slight, dismissive wave as he went. Clive and Ronnie were walking toward me now, in quick, excited steps. Ronnie, who was younger and still occasionally forgot to try to look tough around girls, shook his dollar at me. "A whole dollar, look at that!" he said, and then spun around on his sneakered heel and waved the bill in my face.

"For what? Nightcrawlers?" I asked, knowing that even the very large ones weren't worth more than five cents, and the man did not look like a fisherman.

Ronnie clearly wasn't sure if he was supposed to tell me, and looked to Clive, who took a step toward me and turned his head slightly before saying in a terrible, older-boy voice, "No, stupid. Frogs." I said nothing but pushed past them with my hands tightly wrapped around my handlebars and then climbed on my bike and, when I knew that they couldn't see me anymore, I started pedaling hard in the direction of home. That bucket had been full of frogs, maybe twenty of them, all destined for the man's plates. They had come from the beaver pond, surely. Those were my frogs, and they didn't belong in a pot or a pan or whatever was used to cook a frog. They belonged in their pond. In my pond.

My mother was equally horrified, at least momentarily, when I told her what I had seen, but was more focused on the coffee sputtering away on the gas burner of our stove. She stood with one hand on her hip, wearing an ankle-length flannel nightgown and already smoking an unfiltered Lucky Strike cigarette. The doings of our neighbors were of endless interest to her, even though she lived far above them all in her mind. We were surrounded by people who were all close-knit, intermarried, and endlessly connected. We knew everything about them and they knew everything about us, but we were not a part of the community that was their whole world. We were outsiders, even though my sister and I had been born in Vermont and had lived there our whole, short lives, going to the same schools and stores. We were better than they were; this was made clear to us. My mother had grown up the daughter of an oil man, after all, and had gone to the very best schools in Europe and on the East Coast and was an artist and a bohemian and lived in an old, one-room schoolhouse on the top of a mountain with two tiny daughters by choice, because the beauty and solitude were inspiring and moving and because she wanted to grow her own food and flowers. We had options. Except that now we were here because we had no other place to go. We had been here so long and were so distracted by trying to keep the house from freezing solid that we had started to forget what those options were, and now the money was all gone and we were just as poor as the Rogerses and everyone else who lived on our road year-round. The happy, idealistic band of young people with whom my mother had come here ten years prior had mostly gone home to Connecticut and Virginia, and when they came back to visit us, their new husbands and wives and then children would step out of their shiny cars and stand at the edge of our yard wondering how they were supposed to get to the front door without ruining their shoes.

My sister was sitting at the long bar that divided our kitchen from the rest of our living space, eating toast and petting Plum, the cat that I had been out looking for all morning. I pulled Plum down into my arms and gave her an unwanted hug. She was plump and soft and fine and wriggled away from me and back to my sister and the poorly guarded butter dish. My sister shared my dedication to the protection of The Cute, especially The Baby Cute. We loved frogs, with their wide little eyeballs and glossy green noses poking out of the water at the edge of our beaver pond and their perfect, little webbed fingers. We loved the way they swam and copied them when we were underwater in the deep pool that was at the base of the waterfall behind our house. "Watch me," we would say to each other, one of us on the rock that we used as a jumping-off point and the other already in the water. "And tell me if I'm doing it right." And then we would take a deep breath and dive under and swim like a frog through the crystal-clear water until we reached the edge of the pool where the waterfall was and we would come up for air and look to see what sort of frog-swimming score we had earned. "I would have had my fingers apart," I would shout over the roar of the waterfall, holding my hand up with my fingers spread, "except they aren't webbed enough, so it's better if they are closed."

I had caught a million frogs, but I had let them go. If they were small and young, they almost always peed in your hand from being afraid. Frogs can see shadows with their eyes closed, because their skin is so thin, so you must be very careful not to get between them and the sun. The trick to catching them is to wait for them in the water, with the sun in your face. They will be sitting on the edge of the water, especially if it's morning, warming themselves up. Then you have your sister or your dog startle them from behind so that they leap into the water and start swimming madly. Frogs are not good at making quick turns when they are swimming as fast as they can, so you need only to cup your hands and position them underwater properly, and they will swim right into them. It's very important to let them go right away. They breathe through their skin, and if you get too much of your own skin's oils and dirt on them, they can get very sick.

We knew that the man only came up on weekends and that Ronnie and Clive must have been waiting for him on the road, above the beaver pond. They had probably flagged him down on that Monday morning, and they probably knew what we knew, which was that he would be making the same trip every Monday morning until wintertime. A dollar was a lot of money. In 1975, it bought a gallon of milk and a dozen eggs. It also bought one hundred Tootsie Rolls at the Village Store, ten Popsicles, or two gallons of gas. Ronnie and Clive didn't own the beaver pond, but neither did we. They surely saw its frog population as theirs for the taking, and we saw it as ours to protect.

We knew that we could get to the pond before Ronnie and Clive because they had cows, which meant that they had morning chores. They would be up at dawn, but it would take them at least an hour to finish milking. We did not have anything resembling a chore and needed only to put on our shoes and run out the door. On Sunday night we went to bed in our clothes, which we did most of the time anyway. We found plastic buckets and put them by our bed, next to our shoes, their laces untied and waiting. When the first bit of light came into our room, we bolted out of bed and put them on. I made a double knot in case I had to step into the pond, which had such a thick, muddy bottom that it would suck off a shoe if it wasn't secured tightly. We ran out the front door, past the motionless pile of dark red hair, wool blankets, and cats that was our mother, still sleeping.

We had only to run across our road and through a large, sloping horse pasture to get to the beaver pond. Clive and Ronnie would come through the woods, where there was an overgrown road that began in their gulch. It was the same road that intersected our own, and it was at that intersection that I had seen them the week before selling the frogs. The sun was still coming over the hills and nothing was warm yet; the frogs were all still sleeping in their mud. We lay down on our stomachs in the grass ten feet from the water, with our chins resting on our folded hands, waiting for them to come out of hiding. Soon we could feel the sun hitting our backs and our bare forearms. It became hot quickly, and I could feel the water in my shoes becoming mist. I could hear small noises coming from the water, tiny splashes and plunks, and I knew that they were waking up now and climbing into the tall grass along the edge of the pond to sit in the sun. When I pulled myself up onto my knees to steal a look, two or three frogs leapt back into the water, so I quickly lay down again.

The pond wasn't very deep. Its water was dark and still, and where it began and the pasture and woods ended was hard to discern in most places. The beavers that had built the dam and clogged the small creek and flooded the low-lying area—or at least their descendants—lived on the far, forested edge. There had been trees on either side of the creek before the beavers and before us, but now there were gray, splintery stumps poking up through the water. Sometimes when the pond was frozen over, we walked all the way around it, running mittened hands over the tops of the thin stumps, tracing the lines that the beavers' teeth had made, but the rest of the year you could only reach the water in one small area, which was where we were now. The mud had been packed down here, probably first by the horses that used this pasture every few summers, and then by deer and other animals that came to drink, so that you could reach the edge and even take a few steps in.

When the sun was completely up I stood and walked carefully toward the water with the bucket. I went to the far edge of the muddy beach and stepped into the water and, almost immediately, felt the bottom give way beneath me. It didn't seem to be trying to hold my weight, even for an instant. Silky mud filled my shoes and then climbed up my legs, growing cooler the deeper I sank. I pulled my legs up and moved as quickly as I could toward the center of the muddy beach until I could feel almost solid ground under my feet. The water was just above my knees. I stood in front of a patch of grass that looked like a good place to find frogs and waved to my sister. She took a step toward the pond, and we could hear them begin to jump. I was looking into the sun, which was still low on the horizon, and couldn't see very clearly, but when I looked down, I spotted them in the water, swimming toward me.

Clive and Ronnie came fast, racing each other down the last stretch of road, each with their own bucket. I had a single brown frog in my cupped hands and another swimming toward me when I saw them reach my sister. Clive grabbed her bucket, which was empty, and threw it on the ground. She was frozen, looking up at them. In a few seconds she would be angry; I could see it in the way her shoulders were going up. My sister was smaller than I was and quieter, but she did not like being told what to do, and clearly someone had done just that. Ronnie was coming after me now, and he was wearing high rubber boots that looked ten sizes too big, rising above his knee and making it hard for him to run toward the water. I wanted to turn and swim or run from him, but there wasn't anywhere else to get out of the pond, so instead I had to try to run past him with enough breadth to keep him from pulling me down. I thought of warning him that the ground gave way as soon as you moved away from the beach, because neither of us would be safe if he chased me out there, but his face was so red and angry that I didn't see the point. His hand was suddenly on the edge of my bucket, which now contained my single brown frog, pulling. I looked into his eyes, which were way too close together, and yanked back as hard as I could. He lost his balance, just for an instant, and the frog jumped free and disappeared from sight.

I looked up at my sister in time to see her reach the water, shouting and waving the last of the frogs into the water. Clive had run past her and was making slow progress trying to walk along the muddy edge, hoping to find a patch of frogs that had not been disturbed by the melee, but my sister was screaming so loudly that even the birds on the other side of the pasture were taking flight. Not knowing exactly what advice would motivate a frog to run for safety, she resorted to a repeating loop of phrases like "Stupid boys who smell like cows are trying to get you!" and "Eating frogs is gross!" There could not have been a nonalert living thing within a quarter mile. Unfortunately, a few of the frogs were swimming toward me now, and toward Ronnie. He ruthlessly grabbed one fat brown fellow by his hind legs, and was trying to stuff him into his pocket so that his hands were free to grab another when I reached him and pushed him down. Until now his boots were still above water, but once he went over they filled quickly, and he was having difficulty getting up. I pushed him down again, this time too hard, and turned to see if there were more frogs coming toward us. The water, and the woods around us, was completely silent. Ronnie was calling me horrible, grown-up bad names now, ones I had not even heard before, even though we lived in a profanity-rich environment. And that was when we saw the man in the gray Peugeot, or at least, the gray Peugeot, with a shadow of a man barely visible through the driver's side window, which was rolled up against this beautiful morning and all the dust that its own wheels were making. It was moving very fast, high above us on the other side of the pasture and far beyond shouting distance. Too fast, it seemed, to allow the man to keep his eyes out for two boys selling frogs or plump, slow-moving cats, or anything else that mattered to any of us along that road. Ronnie was almost out of the water now, carrying his boots above his head. He spilled the water out of them and pulled them on, and he and Clive walked away from the pond, toward their old road. They bent their heads together for an instant and then walked into the woods with heavy, wet steps.

My sister and I walked back up through the pasture with our buckets, looking for other things to fill them with. The strawberries were long gone, and the mint was too thick and prickly by now. We left our buckets on the porch because coming into the house with them empty would make our mother think we had failed at something, which we most certainly had not. When we told her what happened, she bent her thin legs at the knees and put her hand on my shoulder. "Listen to me, Tupy," she said. "I don't want you playing with those boys again; they are not nice boys. Do you understand me?"

"Yes, I do," I said. My sister nodded, too.

The following Monday morning was the day before the first day of school. The gray Peugeot had not been seen on the road since the morning we had saved the frogs. Fall was short that year, the leaves were gone by late September, and then there was a bitter, snowless October. Monday mornings were now an endless and often-lost battle to get out of bed and to the third grade. One morning in November we woke up to a thick blanket of snow. We took our sleds to the horse pasture that afternoon and ran them downhill to the beaver pond, where it was silent and peaceful. We knew that buckets and buckets of frogs were buried in the mud below the ice, sleeping soundly until spring.

HOW TO
save a drowning child (part I)

THE RIVER BENEATH CREAMERY Bridge had changed its path at some long-ago point in time, as it carved its way down West Hill through the soil and then the rock. Although it fell in a clean, thick waterfall when I knew it, clearing the rocks behind it by at least two feet and landing in a roaring, thick white blur that obscured the deepest part of the cold, clear pool beneath it, you could see that it had once run down the rock nearby at an angle of forty-five degrees, leaving a long, smooth face that was almost always wet from summer rain and the mist from the falls. And because it sat in the shade of trees that reached out from the riverbanks trying to find sunlight in this deep and narrow gorge, it was nearly always covered in a thin layer of soft moss during the summer. This slide was our favorite of the many things to do at Creamery Bridge and was the sole reason that we wore swimsuits, which made it possible to glide down the rock face and into the river. By the end of any summer, the seats of our suits would be worn and see-through, or ripped completely open.

My mother and her friends favored impractical string biki- nis, often crocheted, or wore nothing at all, but thankfully they stayed mostly hidden in the tall grass that grew on the island formed by the river's divergent paths, just below the falls and the pool. If they swam at all, it was a single jump from a rock, or in my mother's case, a perfect lean dive. Because the water was so unbearably cold, they would quickly climb out and onto the grass, pull on their shirts, and go back to smoking unfiltered Lucky Strike cigarettes and drinking beer from cans. We, their children, all of us small, would stay in the water until we were pulled out, numb and hungry and bruised from stumbling on the rocks and sliding down the moss-covered face. We knew that if we stayed in long enough, we would begin to get used to the temperature and that eventually it would hardly feel cold at all. We would watch our mothers, sitting cross-legged, deep in their serious conversations, arms waving in the air while points were made, not noticing that we were climbing too high on the rocks or swimming too close to the falls, which would push us under and then spit us out. Even if they had wanted to tell us not to do something, we would not have been able to hear them over the rush of the waterfall.

Once my uncle Mike dove from the top of the falls without remembering to take his glasses off, and I spotted them through the clear water as they slowly sank toward the bottom of the pool. I held my breath and dove from the ledge straight down, kicking as hard as I could, until the pressure in my ears and the feeling in my lungs told me to turn around, but not before I man- aged to hook the thin wire frames around my hand as they con- tinued their fall to the bottom, which nobody had ever reached. My lungs had no air left in them when I turned around and swam toward the top. My chest was beginning to ache when I could finally see my uncle's tall frame standing over me just before my numb hand holding on to his glasses broke the surface. He pulled me out with a swift yank, his big calloused hand around my forearm, and studied my face carefully as he wrapped the wire frames around his ears. He was looking at me as though he was seeing me now for the very first time as something other than an annoying child. "Tupy," he said, "thanks."

Fred Fuller, an old friend of my mother and my uncle, moved with his two daughters to Vermont in the summer of 1976. Suddenly, we were with them most of the time, at the schoolhouse and every day at Creamery Bridge. Fred was a tall, thin man with a long beard and a bald spot on the very top of his head. He liked to lounge about in the long grass, naked and pale, as though this was nothing out of the ordinary. I feel certain now, just as I did then, that there are few things as ridiculous to look at as a naked man with a beard. Except maybe a naked man with a beard and a bald spot. Years later, when I was in college, I had an older boyfriend who grew a beard in honor of ski season. I liked him and his warm double bed very much. (In those days, at state colleges at least, if you wanted to sleep in a double bed, you had to date either a professor or someone like Bill, who was still enrolled in college in his mid-twenties partly for the discounted student ski pass.) When Bill got out of bed in the morning, I buried my head under the blankets so that I would not catch sight of him. I assume he thought that I was young and shy and not used to seeing naked men, but the truth was that I had seen more than my fair share of them and did not want to be reminded of Fred Fuller, with his thin arms and silly, proud nudity. Once, I took a quick peek as Bill pulled on his wool socks. Yes. A naked man with a full beard still looked ridiculous, no matter what my age or feelings toward said man.

A naked man with a beard wearing only socks and looking underneath the bed for his long underwear is, by the way, enough to render a girl single no matter how cold the winter or how narrow and dull her dorm-room bed.

Fred was like my mother and my uncle Mike in that he came from a wealthy family and lived, just barely, off the fumes of interest that some well-protected trust fund leaked. He was raising his daughters alone and made it clear to everyone that the more they were exposed to—the more places, the more people, the more adventures—the more well-rounded people he believed they would become. He treated them like adults, which seemed to me to be an excuse for not paying attention to them. It was important to him that his children were seen as different, as special, and this, more than anything, made me feel bad for them because I knew that the only thing children want is to feel that they are the same as other children, that they belong. Fred seemed interested in teaching us things that children would not typically learn and, usually, did not really need to know. One morning, he came to the table where we were sitting in our swimsuits eating spoonfuls of peanut butter straight from the jar for breakfast and showed us, in slow, serious steps with exaggerated movements, how to use a knife to remove the thin bark from a birch twig. "Always cut with the blade *away* from you," he said, "and you won't cut yourself." I tried to imagine needing to remove the bark from a tree and quickly decided that this was not at all something I planned to ever do, and held my breath while I watched the morning sun grow heavier through the window, anxious for this to end so that we could walk together to Creamery Bridge.

Chrissy was just a year older than we were, maybe eight; Meliah was younger, only four or maybe five. Chrissy wore a swimsuit that was sized for a full-grown woman. It sagged in the chest and around her legs. She wanted mostly to lie in the sun with her long, dirty-blond hair fanned out behind her when we were at the Creamery Bridge because she hoped to get a tan and for her hair to lighten. This seemed very boring and time-consuming to my sister and me, who only sat on the rocks in the sun when we had become too cold to form sentences, or to eat, if we had remembered to bring the jar of peanut butter with us, which we rarely had, or if we were hurt and needed a moment to rest. Meliah had a swimsuit that was meant to make her look like she was wearing a tuxedo with no legs or sleeves, but we had just been reading about penguins and mistook it for one. I treaded in deep water in front of her as she stood on the riverbank and explained to her that if she was a penguin, she should be able to swim in even the coldest water, and that she should be able to dive in headfirst, with her arms at her sides. No, she explained to me, that was not possible because she did not know how to swim, and so instead she pulled herself close to the edge and put her feet and ankles into the water. When I put my head under and opened my eyes I could see her toes, curled up against the cold, and the shape of her head and her dark hair.

If we had been told to watch Meliah earlier in the day, we had forgotten. Now it was almost midday and we still had not gone down the slide, because Chrissy could not be convinced that it was fun, so I went there alone. The falls were so loud that I didn't hear them both behind me, and it was not until we were all at the top that I saw them. Chrissy had followed me, and Meliah had followed her, and now Chrissy had turned around to find her small sister, scared and cold, standing in her little penguin suit, at the top of a sheer, slick rock face that ended in deep, cold water. She was shouting for her sister to turn around, to walk back across the top of the face to dry ground, and Meliah seemed to be able to hear or at least understand her, but when she tried to turn around on the steep incline, her hands held out at her sides and her steps wobbly and unsure, she fell and began sliding quickly toward the water. Chrissy's mouth hung open. She was shouting for her father, but I knew that there was no point to this because we were so close to the falls. I had stood in that same spot and watched my mother and my uncle throw their heads back and laugh and shout at one another, without hearing anything at all. I sat down quickly and pushed myself off the top of the incline toward the water with my hands.

I shot past Meliah in the water and had to swim back toward the ledge to reach her. I could see her underwater: Her long black hair was wrapped around her face and neck, covering her eyes, both of her arms were thrashing above her head, and her mouth was filling with water. As soon as she could feel me near her, she grabbed my neck and shoulders and wrapped her arms around them, clinging to me with all four limbs and pulling us both down, then scrambling to push herself on top of me and pushing me down further. I knew nothing about how to save a drowning person. I didn't know that I was supposed to turn her around so that her back was against my side so that she couldn't grab me and pull me under. I didn't know how to pull her with swift kicks or to push her away when I needed to go for air. I only knew how to swim with no air in my lungs, as hard as I could, carrying all of our weight and moving so slowly that I thought we would never reach the edge, until we were close enough to the steep, cut bank that I could push her against it, in time to be swept up by her father, who had finally seen us and had run toward us. I pulled myself onto the bank and spread my tired arms wide and filled my lungs with air.

There was a cold shadow over my face and then a hand on my shoulder. I opened my eyes to see Fred, or at least the part of him that I had been actively avoiding eye contact with, looking me right in the eye. I squeezed my eyes shut and covered my face with both hands and heard him say, as if I needed to be told, "You saved her life, Tupy. Thank you." *Oh, please put some pants on,* I thought, *please, please, please put some pants on.* And then he was gone, carrying Meliah in her little black-and-white penguin suit on his hip, her arms wrapped around his neck, back to the tall grass where the other adults still sat. It was hard for them to know, above the roar of the falls, what had happened, but Fred, Meliah, Chrissy, and my sister and I had all seen.

My mother told me that night that she didn't worry about me when we were at Creamery Bridge because I was a strong swimmer, but I wondered if maybe it was the other way around, if I had become a strong swimmer because there was nobody to worry over me. After that day I began to go swimming alone, without waiting for anyone, or even telling anyone. I wasn't afraid of that place or of the water; instead, being there made me feel strong. Being inside and being alone felt lonely, but being outside, near the water, did not. I would run down the path, and then the gravel road that led from the schoolhouse to the bridge, and jump down the rocky path that dropped along the waterfall to the ledge that juts out still above the cool, clear pool, where Mr. and Mrs. Tyler had had their picnic, in the prettiest spot in all of Vermont, unless of course there happened to be, lounging in the grass as though nothing was out of the ordinary, a naked man with a beard and a bald spot.

HOW TO
help a bird
build a nest

WHEN PEOPLE ASK ME WHO TAUGHT me how to sew or knit or embroider, I usually give credit to my home economics teachers, who were all very good. Or, I say that because we lived much of our childhood without money or other children around and with only one channel on our black-and-white television, we turned to making things out of boredom. These are both true. But what I very rarely admit is that I also have a paternal grandmother—a "Yia Yia," actually, which is the Greek term for "grandmother"—who made it her personal mission not just to teach my sister and me how to do these things but also to push us tirelessly to become child-experts at them, convincing us, or at least me, that our future happiness depended on it.

The den in Yia Yia's house in the suburb of Woodbridge, Virginia, was—and is—dark and clean. On one wall there is a sliding glass door that, if opened, leads into a manicured back-yard dotted with small flowering trees and a chain-link fence that marks the beginnings of other people's lawns and properties. My sister and I had never lived in a suburb, where the houses were only shown from the front, but we had seen them on television and we thought that they were happy places. Especially odd to me was that you could stand in your backyard and look right into the backsides of other homes, which was the side where you hid the parts of your life that you didn't want passersby to see, like broken things waiting to be fixed, and laundry. It didn't make sense to me that you would want to hide these things from the strangers who drove by but that you would let your neighbors see them so clearly. We could see straight into kitchens where heavyset ladies with thick arms and legs worked long, unsmiling hours in sleeveless shirts and bare feet and sometimes in their robes and curlers, or sat at their kitchen tables with their brows resting in their propped-up hands, worrying over a piece of mail or children who had not come home on time. It seemed uncivilized to us, even though the homes and lawns were manicured and their inhabitants respectable. In Vermont, we had acres— no, miles—because when we walked from our house to the river or into the woods, we could never know at what point we had left our own property, because there were no chain-link fences and because it didn't matter. We were surrounded by other large or forgotten properties and forests that didn't seem to belong to anybody, and we were just walking through them anyway. When we did stumble upon a driveway or a house, we turned away from it because we understood that it was private.

But in Woodbridge, you always knew whose property you stood on. You could see clearly where your grass met someone else's grass, and it was impossible not to compare and judge the differences between them and everything else in sight. I watched my grandparents' neighbors trim their lawns and shrubs against the chain-link fencing that marked their property line with what seemed like a special attention.

Yia Yia saw our one-room schoolhouse once, when she and

Grandpa came to collect my sister and me for a visit. My grandfather was polite and warm toward my mother, whose family he had admired, and he hid his disapproval of our living situation admirably. I loved him for a lot of reasons, but especially for that. They stayed just long enough to look around the single room that was our kitchen, our living room, and our mother's bedroom. My grandmother asked if we'd had breakfast, and my mother told her that we had each had some yogurt. Then, in a matter of minutes, we were sitting together on the long, clean bench seat in the back of their monstrous lemon-colored Cadillac on our way to Woodbridge. I don't remember saying goodbye to our mother, and from the inside of the car, we could not see her standing in the doorway, waving to us, but we knew that she was there and that she was alone now and wouldn't see us again for weeks. "Yogurt," spat my grandmother, to my grandfather but also loudly enough for us to hear clearly over the roar of the air conditioner, not thirty feet from the driveway, "is no breakfast." He was silent, the back of his head not even nodding in response.

We stopped just once, when it was dark, at a motel where Yia Yia took off our clothes and scrubbed us clean in water almost too hot to stand, holding our heads underneath the faucet to rinse the shampoo from our hair with powerful, gnarled hands that looked as though they belonged to a woman twice her age and twice her size. Our skin was pink and raw when she finally let us step out to be powdered, coated with her adored Jean Naté, and dressed in clean, new pajamas, purchased at her beloved PX. Whatever clothing we were wearing or had brought with us would disappear while we slept, and by the time we had come back to Vermont, we would have new clothing, matching except for color and size—I was already five or six inches taller and much rounder than my twin sister—and new shoes. Then she sat each of us down and told us to sit on our hands and look straight ahead as she combed our thick, tangled hair. When it was smooth, she pulled a knitting needle from her bag and drew a line with its tip from the middle of our foreheads to the nape of our necks to make a perfect part, then braided each side. She took her scissors and trimmed our bangs, which my mother had cut haphazardly with dull shears without much attention to evenness and which always looked like a smile with missing teeth, and, finally, she cut the bottom of each braid so that their tips were thick and flat, like the bristles on a vegetable brush. Then she tucked us into a double hotel bed and turned off the light, and I lay in the dark wondering at the smell of my hair and my skin and missing the cats that usually came into our beds at home.

My sister loved the structure, the sense of being cared for in such a way and protected, the new pajamas and the evenly cut bangs. She knew more certainly than I did that we were, in our daily lives, missing out on something and that children needed more constant grooming and caring for than what we were given. I was less sure. My sister and I were different in many ways, including how we looked. I took after my mother's family, who were all very fair and blue-eyed and didn't like to admit they were wrong or weak. My sister looked a lot like our father's mother, who was from Greece. This similarity was a source of special pride for my grandmother, who thought of Christie as the daughter that she didn't have but had always hoped for. Christie also had a hot temper and loved people and things with a frighteningly passionate attachment. When her collection of stuffed animals outgrew her bed, she started sleeping on the floor rather than ban any of them. She tried very hard to hide her favoritism toward her favorite toy, a stuffed mouse, especially around mine, a stuffed elephant. She was sensitive to situations that seemed dangerous, quick to hold the adults in our life responsible for creating them, and appreciative of the respite that visits to Woodbridge afforded us. In turn, my grandmother favored my sister in the ways that grandparents are able to do, unapologetically, blatantly.

Yia Yia had been what my mother called a war bride, married at sixteen to my grandfather, who had joined the army at fifteen and gone to Greece as an American soldier. She told us horrifying stories of her childhood in occupied Greece, stories of starvation and death and always ending with the hand of God reaching down to punish those who had been most cruel. "We had no food to eat so my mother give me all her gold jewelry to take to the wealthy family in town, to trade with them for the flour and sugar, but they trick me and what did I know? I was only a little girl, just barely older than you are now. They gave me sacks of marble dust and so we were starving, but now the jewelry is gone, too, and I cried for my mother and my brothers and sisters." There would be a pause here, an opportunity for the listener to react, and then she would start again with her eyebrows suddenly meeting in the middle and her eyes widened: "But then, after the war ended, the whole family was walking down the street together in their fine clothes, and a bus came fast down the street and ranned over them, the whole family, and smashed them all to DEATH!" Here she would add a forceful hand movement, clapping one palm against the other or down onto the table, and pause, hands landing on her thighs and throwing herself back in her chair before her story's moral was revealed. "Now you tell me there is no God!" She made it hard to disagree.

This God of hers, however, seemed more interested in revenge than in keeping terrible things from happening in the first place. Yia Yia kept an especially bloody crucifix on her bedroom wall and explained to us why it was important for us to thank Jesus, because we had killed him, and God was angry about that. She tried to teach us about her religion, but her English wasn't very good and her stories were too frightening, and eventually God, in my mind, began to resemble Lex Luthor, and I knew that it was probably time to stop listening.

Yia Yia read tea leaves, but mostly to satisfy her own curiosity rather than as a service. She would not tell guests that she was peering into their future as she slid the teacups in front of them, which often caught them by surprise since they neither requested nor drank tea. When they would leave her kitchen, she would tell us what she had seen. "Poor Mrs. Buchko," she would report to us. "Her daughter, she will never marry, because she moved to the city and now is a Bad Girl." The tea leaves never seemed to deliver good news, and most disappointments that would befall her guests had one thing in common: They could be blamed on a Bad Girl.

Yia Yia had kept her handmade wedding dress and showed it to us once, not letting us touch it, but pointing to it, wrapped in thick clear plastic and stowed on a high shelf in the hall closet. Then she turned to my sister and said in her thick accent, "Someday, Christine, you will be married and you will wear my dress." My sister was silent.

"What about me?" I asked, because that's what you are in the habit of saying when you are a twin and one of your set is offered something—anything—by anyone. She broke into a knowing smile, as though we were exchanging knock-knock jokes and I had just delivered the question that would prompt her punch line, which she delivered to my sister triumphantly. "Heather won't be able to wear my dress; she will be too fat."

Our grandfather doted on us, showing us an affection that nobody else, not his three grown sons or grandson, had ever known from him, their soldier father. When he came home, we would run to the door, and he would pick us up and love us. We had never lived in a house with a man who came home every day at the same time, but we had seen them on television enough to know what to do. In the evenings we would both curl up with him, one under each arm, in a giant green leather chair and watch *Gilligan's Island* and have whatever we liked to eat. He loved us exactly the same, the way our mother did.

But Grandpa would be at work by the time we woke up in the morning, and we would be alone with Yia Yia, who seemed to always be cleaning and cooking. She would serve us a heavy breakfast in her small, immaculate kitchen and then announce that it was time for us to move downstairs, into the den. The idea of playing inside when it was perfectly nice outside seemed strange to me, even when I was just four or five, because summers in Vermont were so fleeting and wonderful, you wouldn't waste a moment of them indoors, where you would be trapped for months on end come winter. Yia Yia, on the other hand, felt that outdoors was where you went when you needed to hang laundry or walk to the car or take a photo in your matching dresses on her front stoop, which was framed by enormous, structurally insignificant Gothic columns. She also believed that childhood was not so much about playing as about learning how to be good at being an adult. We were to spend our waking hours on the floor of the den, where a large waterproof plastic mat would be laid down and the curtains drawn to protect the color of her precious wall-to-wall carpeting, practicing our homemaking skills.

This, she explained, would be how we would win good husbands, with our knitted afghans and scarves and ability to mend shirts and hem pants. In my case especially, this was my only hope. My sister was beautiful, with dark hair and shiny skin. She looked Greek, even as a child. We were twins, and I was taller, but she had been shaving her legs for two years before I needed to wear a shirt, much less a bra. I was too tall and too thick and too messy and apparently unavoidably destined for obesity, but Yia Yia had indicated that all of that could be overlooked if I could make a man happy with my skills as a homemaker. I threw myself into the task, relieved to finally receive some clear instruction on the mystery of how to make somebody—anybody—love me, and believing without question everything she told me.

She brought us an old, large stuffed bear, bigger than either of us, and taught us to knit hats and scarves for it and to crochet afghans made from granny squares to lay over it. It did not sit up on its own, so we laid it on its back on our plastic mat and tended to it like a giant, silent baby, which is what I came to imagine a husband to be, not ever having lived in a house that had one. I endeavored to knit a scarf that was long enough to reach her across-the-street neighbors' front door but ran out of yarn when it was about twelve feet long and was devastated when Yia Yia claimed to find a small slipped stitch. "It is no good. It will fall apart like garbage," she said, pushing it back into my hands and pointing at it with a shaking finger, commanding me to "take it all out and do it again." My sister had no patience for these lessons and abandoned me to care for our pretend husband alone in favor of the sofa and the remote-controlled television and constant supply of snacks that Yia Yia brought us. She wasn't worried; she would be thin and beautiful and very popular at the

Greek festivals that Yia Yia promised to take us to when we were older (this actually turned out to be true; as adults, Christie and I went to a Greek festival, where a small troupe of dancers circled her as part of their performance, as though she were a deity). But I was taking things even more seriously after this setback.

I moved on to crochet, which seemed to me to be more sculptural and free-form, its mistakes less obvious. I made dozens, maybe hundreds, of granny squares and sewed them together into an ugly poncho. I collected needles and hooks in every size. I learned to shorten and lengthen a pair of pants with an invisible, flexible stitch, sitting next to Yia Yia on the sofa, my face so close to her elbow that I can still smell her perfume when I hand-sew a hem. I presented to her knitted slippers, made with a pattern that I had designed myself (she never used patterns; only lazy people needed patterns), and handkerchiefs made from scraps of fabric and embroidered with my initials, their edges rolled and stitched carefully, but with a child's hand and patience. Every finished project was brought to her in her kitchen, as she ironed or cooked while watching her soap operas, which kept her head happily nodding in disapproval most of the morning, but nothing I made ever met her approval or made her smile.

I left Woodbridge with plastic bags full of cheap synthetic yarns, needles, hooks, and pins, my determination to become a good wife stronger than ever. We spent that winter in the schoolhouse surrounded by yarn and fabric, some of it from Yia Yia and her PX and some of it from my mother, who could also knit and sew and embroider. She came from a family of artists and craftspeople, collectors of textiles and artwork, fashionable, worldly upper-class women who could design and make complicated and beautiful things with their hands in their leisure. We knitted up every bit of yarn that we had and then unraveled what we didn't love and knitted with it again. Then we took apart old moth-eaten sweaters and dirty scarves and the odd, pointy slippers that Yia Yia sent us every winter that were neither pretty nor warm enough for our house, and knitted and crocheted sweaters and blankets for the cats, the mice, and the imaginary family of house gnomes who lived under our potbelly woodstove. We made slippers and hats for Mouse and Elephant to keep them warm on nights when there wasn't room for them under our blankets. We moved on to more elaborate costumes and little shrouds in which to wrap the small mammals and birds that our cats hunted and brought into our house to die, building dioramas from shoeboxes to display them in dramatic poses, held by the magic of rigor mortis, and in costume in a variety of scenes. Greek tragedies and Romeo and Juliet were favorites. It was days of snowbound fun, at least until our mother realized, led by the stench of many small deaths coming from our room, that we were storing dead animals—and their wardrobes and accessories—like Barbie dolls under our beds and threw them all out.

Our tomcat brought home an injured blue jay that seemed to prefer our warm house to his winter nest and settled into a wide perch at the top of one of our windows. I thought I recognized him as the same blue jay that I had seen days before, collecting the bits of fox fur from the barbed wire fence that bordered the pasture across our road to build his nest. We were desperate for him to love us, to stay with us and let us feed him from our hands and perch on our shoulders. We knitted him a bright red scarf out of wool embroidery thread, using toothpicks with beads stuck onto the ends for needles. When it was finally finished and painstakingly cast off, late one night at the foot of our mother's bed, we sat together in the dark plotting how we would tie it around his tiny neck—surely he would love it once he realized how much warmer he was with it on—but when we woke up, he was gone. My mother had been waiting for the injuries from his capture to heal before she let him go.

"But we made this for him," I said, "and we were going to give it to him today!"

"We can leave it outside for him, and he'll see it and take it to his nest and use it as a blanket, I'm sure of it," was her response.

We climbed into our winter clothing with our small, thick mittens and pushed open our heavy wooden door. We found a low branch and hung the scarf from it, loosely because birds don't have thumbs to untie things with, and we went back inside, where we sat pressed against the window, watching for our blue jay. Surely he would find it. Night came and we went to bed, but when we woke up we ran to the window and saw that it was gone. Our mother assured us that he must have come for it, and we agreed, as we could see no footprints in the snow underneath it, but when the snow melted in the spring, I found it in the muddy grass beneath the tree where it had hung and I buried it there, digging a hole in the still partly frozen ground with a stick, so that Christie would not stop believing that there was a blue jay somewhere wearing a red scarf, or using it to wrap up his babies, and who was our true friend.

When we eventually left the schoolhouse, we went to live with our father in Virginia. Yia Yia was only an hour away, and she wanted us to stay with her and Grandpa every weekend. On that first Friday afternoon, Yia Yia pulled us into her home as though she were saving us, scrubbed us again as thoroughly and roughly as if we were rusted metal, cut our hair as short as it had ever been, hung small gold chains with crosses around our necks, and drove us to Tyson Corners to have our ears pierced without first consulting us or either of our parents. My sister would not let the teenager with the chewing gum in her mouth hold the piercing gun up to the side of her head unless I went first. I didn't want pierced ears or the little gold beads on sharp posts that I had been pushed to choose, but Christie sort of did, even if the means terrified her, so I closed my eyes and pretended that I had barely felt it. Later that night we argued over something—we only fought when we were around adults who loved us unevenly—and when she pulled my hair she tore one of the little gold studs out. I could not keep the injured lobe clean enough to avoid infection and, after weeks of trying, gave up on having pierced ears altogether, with total indifference.

We spent almost every weekend with Yia Yia when we lived in Virginia, and our lessons in handwork continued. Yia Yia and I grew further apart, but Grandpa and I were a team. He loved us and cared for us in a way that no other adult had, and when I was with him I felt smart and pretty and good. Then our father, who was by then only thirty and barely able to make a living, much less care for two little girls without so much help from his parents, was accepted into the University of California, Santa Cruz, and announced that when we came back to him in the fall, it would be to a new home in California. Our grandparents were devastated. We spent a final weekend with them, during a muggy early June, and ate a dinner of Greek pot roast on their upstairs terrace, looking down over the patchwork of lawns all separated by chain-link fences. After the sun went down you could not see the fences anymore, but you could still make out the perfect boundaries between properties because of the varying color and shortness of the grass, still visible in the near dark.

We spent the summer in Vermont with our mother and then,

when fall came, boarded a plane and met our father in California. He married not long after, to a woman who barely tolerated us, and had a son. This wife and I could not stand one another, and a few years later, just before I turned fourteen and as our annual visit to see our mother the following summer came to an end, I enrolled in high school in Vermont. My mother had no phone, so I had no way of telling my father that I wasn't coming back; I just didn't get on the plane. My stepmother was elated; my father and I wouldn't speak for years. Christie stayed in California with our father, barely tolerated by his new wife, but becoming like a second mother to his new son, our little half-brother. She put herself through college, married when we were only twenty-one, and had three children. I came back to the West Coast after college to be closer to her and her growing family. When her oldest daughter, who was the first child that I loved, was a small and pretty thirteen, she was finally allowed to get her ears pierced. We drove to the shopping mall, where a gum-chewing teenager put a velvet-covered board dotted with metal beads in front of her. I pushed her to get the silver, not the gold. She wanted so badly to have pierced ears, to be officially a teenager, but when she saw the gun, she froze. I still didn't have holes in my ears, all of those years since that drive to Tyson Corners, so I offered to go first.

A few winters ago, my friend Denyse gave me a remarkable gift. I don't know where she found it, but she sent me a ball of unwashed wool, tied up loosely in string, meant to be hung in the branches of a tree. The idea is that birds of all kinds will find it and pull bits of the wool through the strings and fly back to their nests, where they will weave it between the sticks and grasses. I hung it on a high branch with the help of two little girls who were far better tree climbers than I, now almost an old person, and have watched from my kitchen window as it grows smaller and smaller, disappearing, bit by bit, into my woods.

Bird netting, which is designed to protect trees and their fruit from birds, works here to enclose a small ball of the perfect nesting material—wool roving or fleece. You'll need a small ball of wool roving or fleece, a 2' x 2' (61 x 61 cm) square of netting, string for closing, and at least 30' (9 m) rope for hanging. ● To begin, make a loose, round ball of wool and place it in the center of the square of netting. Gather up the edges of the netting, then the corners, and use string to bind closed the top end. To hang, tie one end of a long rope around a rock or other heavy item. Make sure the rope is secure. Stand directly under the branch where you want to hang your nest bundle (make sure it is a place where it can be reached by a bird standing on a nearby branch, as larger birds won't be able to balance on it long enough to pull bits of wool out), then take 10 steps backward. Throw the rock over the branch, leaving a loose pile of rope in front of you. This may take a few attempts. When you have succeeded and the rope is over the branch and the rock is safely on the ground again, remove the rock from the rope's end and replace it with your wool bundle, tying it securely. Use the other end of your rope to hoist it into place, then tie the loose end of the rope around the tree's trunk, knotting it in a way that can be easily undone.

HOW TO
make a warm bed

WE HAD BEEN TRYING TO GET Beth Johnson's mother to let Beth spend the night at the schoolhouse since the first day of first grade. The Johnsons were really more friends of my mother's parents than of my mother, even though Beth's mom was close in age to my own. Beth and her parents and her four brothers and sisters lived in the same resort community that my grandparents did, a place called Alpine Haven. Alpine Haven consisted of forty or so chalet-style homes, all chocolate and white with flower boxes and stucco foundations, nestled into the forest on the backside of a ski area that served mostly upper-middle-class French Canadians. The Johnsons lived at Alpine Haven year-round, which almost nobody did, and they sent their kids to the local public schools. Beth and my sister and I were in the same grade.

Beth's mother's name was Margaret. She wore her auburn hair long and had thick, lumpy eyelashes. She dressed in brightly colored pantsuits with bell-bottoms and shirts with wide, pointy collars and ankle boots with heels. Margaret claimed proudly not to be a "working mother" but made a tidy little income collecting used children's clothing and selling it to women like my grandmother, who would conspire with her to organize ridiculous, outdated wardrobes for my sister and me and our cousins. When we visited her house for tedious trying-on sessions, she made great efforts to steer us away from her velvet turquoise sectional sofa, which apparently was very expensive and important. Once, when she walked my grandmother to her waiting car and left us for a moment, we ran to it and sat on it, just wearing our underpants. "It's like it's made of bunnies!" my sister said to me. "Lots and lots of bunnies!" I felt certain that our grandmother was allowed to sit on it, but I had never seen her or anyone else do so. We saw the way that Beth's mother treated our grandmother, with respect and sweetness, and then the way she treated our mother and us, and suspected, based on the difference, that she was pretending to be a good person but that actually she was not.

The Johnsons went to church. A lot. They talked about God all the time, about what he wanted us to be doing and not doing and how he was always watching. Sometimes, on Sundays in the summertime, Beth would walk from her house to the Alpine Haven swimming pool, still dressed in her church clothes, with her long, thick auburn hair tied up out of her face with ribbons. She would sit on the steps that led to the pool and watch us swim with her chin resting in her hands. We knew that she wasn't allowed to do anything fun on Sundays because she was supposed to be resting. We would tell her that nobody was watching and that she could at least take off her shoes and kneesocks, and that she would still be resting, but she couldn't be persuaded. I felt certain that she was wrong. I was happy to believe in—even appreciate—a God at the age of six, because at that point in my life everything about the natural world seemed to be the product of intelligent design: the perfect clear pool beneath the waterfall just behind our house, the tiny, sweet strawberries that covered acres of horse meadow across our dirt road, the apple trees made for climbing and hanging from by one's knees, the cool green grass that grew and grew and grew. We saw spring happen every year, under our feet, bringing with it daffodils and soft kittens born in my sweater drawer and wild roses. All of this seemed miraculous to me and, because science had not yet wrecked it for all of us, like definite proof of God. I didn't know yet that the mossy trail worn in the mud and grass that led to the river from our yard had been made by hundreds of people before me, or that wise men had long ago forced apple trees to grow small so that their fruit could be easily reached, or that the roses in our woods, now wild but once cultivated, were all that remained of a cabin that had burned down a century before. I didn't know that there was an explanation for almost everything. I thought it was extremely silly of Margaret Johnson to think that God had time to keep track of what each and every person was doing during the weekend. If God wanted me to do anything differently, he didn't mention it, and based on what I knew about his work, he didn't really seem like the type of person who would be angry at me for going swimming on a Sunday, especially a really muggy one.

My sister and I didn't know that it was the Johnsons who sent the missionaries to our house, but my mother must have suspected it. We liked the two nice ladies who started to appear regularly in our driveway in their clean little car—they brought us books and played games with us. Their names were Anna and Hannah, which we thought was a riot. We could never remember which one was which. We did impressions of them after they left that made my mother laugh so hard that no noise came out.

Hannah had a huge bottom, so my sister would put on a pair of our mother's wool tights, stuff a pillow into the back of them, stand on the coffee table, and try to remember one of the many pious sayings that Hannah and Anna loved to use. "Treat undo others better than they treat you!" and "Never do anything today that can be put off until never!" My mother had wanted to shoo them away at first, but we assured her that we liked them, and we didn't have many visitors, so they were, at worst, a novelty. She began to look at them as babysitters, and when they came over, she would put a glass of something in one hand and a lit cigarette in the other and step backward out the front door, pushing it open with her elbow. She would sit on the porch or work in the garden, and she wouldn't come back until she heard their car pull away.

It must have been the missionaries who finally convinced Margaret Johnson to let Beth spend the night at our house. We had begged and pleaded and asked and demanded for more than a year, and even when Margaret Johnson finally said yes, we knew that she was wary, but we thought we had finally worn her down. We could see the concern in her face when she brought Beth, holding her small, rolled-up sleeping bag under one arm, and they both looked around inside our little one-room schoolhouse, with a small bedroom and bathroom added onto the back. Our ceilings were very high, and there were big windows on every wall with wavy glass in the panes. My mother's bed was in one corner, near the potbelly woodstove that was our one source of heat. In another corner was our kitchen, which was really just a stove and a sink and a long wooden bar that someone had taken out of an old saloon. The rest of the space was filled with furniture that had been cast off and collected and with my mother's paintings, plants, and cats. Our blankets and dishes were from

Mexico, where we had lived for a while, and our chairs were rattan and from Indonesia, where my mother had spent much of her childhood. Margaret and Beth looked around, not saying a word. We could see that Beth was scared—we were children and knew those signs—but we pulled her in and made her laugh and showed her where Teddy slept under the stove and made her touch his tail, which was as hot as could be, and we made spaghetti and threw the noodles against the wall to see if they were ready, and then we climbed into my mother's bed to watch *The Waltons* on our tiny black-and-white TV under stacks of wool blankets with the cat nearly suffocating us. It became very, very cold, and my mother added more wood than usual to the fire. We wondered if Beth was allergic when she started sneezing but decided that it was just the dust that she wasn't used to. My mother made us Swiss Miss cocoa, which she never did, and we all fell asleep almost as soon as the boring news came on. My mother put us into our beds, tucking Beth in next to my sister, probably because I was so much bigger and there would be more room in her bed. Then she sat near the stove drinking wine, knitting the second mitten of a pair for me.

We woke up in the arms of firemen. I could feel something scratchy and cold against my face, and when I opened my eyes I saw the chin and shoulder of a man with a big hat on. He was wearing enormous gloves and a coat that felt like it was made of metal. There was a man in front of me who seemed to be wearing the same kind of coat, and resting on one of his shoulders was the sleeping face of my sister; on the other shoulder was Beth, her eyes open, big, and full of tears. There was a noise all around us, a thundering, cracking sound, like a cat stuck inside a paper bag, or a rushing waterfall, and the air felt like it did when you were sitting in front of a bonfire and the wind suddenly shifted, and the thick rope of white smoke went into your face. The firemen were walking fast, and suddenly we were outside, looking up at a clear sky full of stars and half a moon and the thick gray smoke that was billowing from our roof. The air was clean but so bitterly cold that we choked on it until tears streamed down our faces. They put us into the fire truck's front seat with our blankets over us and the heat blowing on us. The truck faced the road, but I could look past my sister and Beth and see through the window as my mother and our neighbors dragged everything that we owned through our front door and into the snow. The passenger-side door would open every few minutes and a fireman would toss a frightened cat into our laps. Plum, our plump favorite, clung to my chest with her front claws. I buried my face in her neck and smelled soot and smoke, but not the kind that comes from a woodstove.

It was so cold that night that the firemen's equipment wouldn't work properly. They ran hoses from their truck to our well, where they tried to pump water into their pressurized systems, but the hoses were too long because our house was too far from the road, and they kept freezing. By the time they were able to spray water onto our roof, most of it had burned away. My mother had caught the fire very early when she heard what she thought were raccoons on our roof. She pulled on her boots and went outside to check, and when she looked up at our chimney, she saw that a cinder had found its way up our flue and had landed on the roof, which was on fire. We had no phone, so she ran in her nightgown and unlaced boots down our icy dirt road to our neighbor's house, where she called the volunteer fire department.

We had only been in the truck a few minutes when Margaret Johnson appeared before us. Our road had been purposely blocked just before our driveway by one of the fireman's cars, so she was on foot when she reached the truck where we sat. She appeared suddenly, running into the headlights of the fire truck, out of the darkness like a ghost, tears streaming down her face, her long hair trailing behind her. Beth began to cry again as soon as she saw her, and then she was climbing over my sister and putting her arms around her mother's neck and leaving us and her blanket behind. Margaret didn't look at us or ask if we were OK. She didn't find my mother or speak to anyone. She pulled Beth up onto her chest and walked back toward her car, burying her face in Beth's neck and holding her as tightly as she could. We could see Beth's face over her shoulder, moving away from us and finally fading into the darkness. It wasn't until that moment that I realized that we would not be going back into our house and waking up to bowls of cereal in our pajamas and then going back to our pretend games on the wood floor next to the woodstove. It may not have been possible for my mind to grasp what had happened to our home, but the sadness that our sleepover was over was paralyzing. Plum moved off my lap and into the warm spot that remained. We were there for a long time and finally fell asleep curled up together, me and my sister and the cats.

I do not know what my grandparents paid Margaret Johnson to invite us to live with her while our house was being repaired, but it must have been a lot. There was surely some sort of payment made, and perhaps some pressure from Margaret's church, which was already invested in and familiar with our situation. Still, why my mother agreed is the bigger mystery. At first we were excited about the spacious rumpus room, with its enormous color television, but then we learned that it was only to be watched at certain times, and under certain conditions, and with our feet on the floor and not on the couch, and with no snacks or other food. It was to remain, it seemed to me, rumpus-free. And when someone changed the channel, you did not shout "GOD, why did you do THAT?" the way you did in our house, because God's name was not to be used "in vain," a term that I wished someone would explain to me. Meals were served with great ceremony and what felt to us like sadness and guilt, and with their own set of bizarre regulations. Every room had its own set of rules, so the easiest thing to do was to just stay in one place. My sister and I would sit on my mother's borrowed bed in the basement and listen for mealtime announcements, given over the house's intercom system. Beth seemed to avoid us, until her mother prompted her to give us each a gift of a new hairbrush and a package of barrettes. She asked if we would like her to show us how to put up our hair at each corner, over our ears, the way she wore hers, and when we politely declined, she left the room in relief.

Our mother was going up to our house, which sat lonely and cold with tarps thrown over the holes in the roof, almost every day to feed our cats, who were not allowed at the Johnsons' house. We convinced her to let us go with her once, by promising not to let it make us sad. When we got there, Plum came running out the front door, which was now propped permanently open with snow surrounding it on all sides, to greet us with loud purrs and by wrapping herself around our ankles. I wanted to sit on the ground and let her curl up in my lap and scratch her head, but I was wearing a winter coat that didn't belong to me—it was from Margaret's collection of clothing that was for sale and we had not paid her for it yet, so I was afraid to get it dirty.

Margaret Johnson woke up my sister and me on the second Sunday morning of our stay and told us that we were going to church. Appropriate clothing—more secondhand pieces, carefully selected and no doubt invoiced—was laid out on the foot of the bed for us. The car ride was long and dull, and the fact that my mother was not present was the main topic of conversation. "Sometimes," Margaret said to me, suspiciously sweetly, "the child must choose a different path than his parent, and hope that they will follow their love toward him." I had no idea what little boy Margaret was referring to. Beth led us into a Sunday-school class, which is where I tuned out completely. When it was finally over and we filed out into the hallway and were standing among a hundred adult legs, all in trousers and skirts and brown shoes, my sister grabbed my arm. "Look!" she said, "It's Hannah and Anna!" pointing up at the pair, who were just a few feet away, with husbands and children—one of whom had been sitting next to me in Sunday school. We looked at each other with the same wide-eyed expression, realizing suddenly that we had fallen for their tricks; they had never mentioned any children or church or knowing the Johnsons. We had been led here, and here was where we most certainly did not belong. My sister took Margaret's arm in her small hand and stared at her coldly. "I want to see my mother," she said. It was not the voice of a frightened or hurt child, and it wasn't meant as a suggestion.

Our mother was waiting for us when we got back to the Johnsons' house. We took off our church clothes and laid them back down onto the bed and gathered together what little we had brought with us. I placed the hairbrush that Beth had given me on the bed with the clothing but kept the barrettes. We never said thank you or good-bye; we just climbed into our little car, and before the vents were even blowing hot air, we were on our way into town and then up our hill. The trip seemed so effortless, with no one to stop us or warn us or even notice us. Plum was so happy to see us that she kept falling over from purring too hard. We pulled the mattress off our mother's bed and dragged it to a place on the floor that seemed dry and protected and flipped it over to reveal the side that had not been damaged by smoke and water. We pulled the Mexican wool blankets out of the tall wicker baskets that they had been stuffed into during the fire. They smelled like soot and smoke but now also like home and like Plum. It was still very cold but not quite the middle of winter anymore. We could almost imagine spring happening now, and we could hear a small but steady dripping of melting snow off the roof and on the tarps that kept the snow from falling into our house, at least until the sun went down. Then we piled the blankets high on the mattress and curled up together, my sister and I on either side of my mother, and lay on our backs looking up through the wavy glass of our tall windows at our sky. We were home.

HOW TO
swim a horse

MY UNCLE MIKE WAS MARRIED when I was twelve. His wife, Mary, was beautiful, a dark-haired, blue-blooded woman who was still a student at Bennington College when they met and only twenty-four when they married. When she moved onto the mountain, she brought some horses with her. My grandparents, who believed in nonteam sports like riding, skiing, tennis, and ballet, were convinced, without much effort, that my cousins, sister, and I should learn to ride from her. My grandfather once told me that women who took ballet had the finest posture, and he felt certain that girls who played field hockey did not make good wives and that women who were not fearful of horses were not fearful of anything. And so Mary raked out a rough schooling ring on the one piece of level ground that dropped away into steep pasture and then into the valley a mile below us, and assigned us each a day of the week, which was when we would come for an hour-long lesson, rain or shine, for which my grandmother paid.

There were trails on the mountain, too, including one that climbed all the way up to and then snaked along the ridgeline, spitting you out on the other side of the steep creek that carved the valley between our mountain and the one to its south, but at a point so high in the watershed that you crossed thousands of tiny streams instead of one rushing one, which is when I learned how a river is made. There was a dark forest trail that crossed a steep gulch via something called a slide, which is when a hillside is so steep and the soil is so loose that the only way down is to give the horse his head—basically give him control—lean back as far as you can, and let him make his own way, sometimes stepping with cautious and jarring steps, and sometimes not moving his legs at all but just sliding on all four feet, with his hind legs bent and his nose straight down. The trails, though, were only open to us for the longer rides that were a reward for surviving the grueling hours in the ring for weeks at a time.

Mary's father had been a cavalry something or other, and she believed, as he had, that until you could post (which means lifting yourself a few inches off the horse's back repeatedly at a certain point during a trot, to avoid the heaviest impact of each stride) bareback, using only the strength of your knees and practiced timing, you didn't deserve a saddle or stirrups. Mary would put a dollar bill between my knee and the horse and lunge me in circles around the ring for what seemed like full days, and if the dollar was still there when she finally let the horse slow to a walk, it was mine to keep. Mary's sharp commands and short temper kept me focused, and after two summers, when she proclaimed me her star student (not much of an achievement, really, since by then my cousins and sister had abandoned their weekly lessons, and it was just me who still showed up), I was hooked.

Mike and Mary's horses seemed a mismatched lot, a mix of

breeds and temperaments, but each with its own character and
purpose. Butternut was the Morgan, the beauty: Tall, sturdy,
quiet, and blond, she was Mike's favorite. She had come from
a very fancy barn called Taproot in Shelburne, Vermont, where
Morgans were bred to perfection. Morgans are meant to possess
the most athletic qualities of a horse sized for riding, with the
temper, sturdiness, and work ethic of a draft horse. Butternut
was a magnificent athlete, but she did not like to take orders.
For this reason, she had been pulled from the breeding stock at
Taproot and found her way to Mike, for whom she was a perfect
match. He would let her run her heart out on the last mile home,
and when you saw them from Mike's porch coming up the mountain on the dirt road just after the sun had set, from a half-mile
away—her in a wild gallop and him with both hands thrown
forward, almost touching her neck, his tall, lean form balanced
in the saddle, almost motionless—you held your breath.

Bucky was the old schooling horse. He and I had what you
might call a May-December love affair. I loved him in that way
that a girl can love a horse or a dog or a kitten, in that painfully smothering way that had been practiced on stuffed animals
and does not consider what unrequited love could possibly feel
like. I would stare into Bucky's eyes for solid minutes, hoping
to make some sort of mental or magical communicative connection, certain that I was getting somewhere. "You're making him
nervous," Mike would say. "He's nearly blind, you know, you're
just a big nosey blur to him."

I stood on my toes and whispered into Bucky's ear as I gave
it a scratch. "It's OK, Bucky, I'll be your eyes."

"He's deaf too, Tupy," Mike said, clearly annoyed and
watching me carefully now. "Deaf as cheese." I would climb
onto his back with just my jeans and rubber boots on and lie on

his neck, with my arms wrapped around him, my bare chest on his bristly neck where I had torn bits of mane out by the fistful during our lessons. I especially loved to do this when it was raining, which it did on many afternoons, closing my eyes and feeling the steam coming off him and searching for that cosmic connection through his coat. He would wait until I was almost asleep and then reach down suddenly as though he wanted to eat some grass and then quickly take a step back, and I would slide forward and off and land in a pile at his feet, with a thin coat of wet horse hair, some of it gray, on my chest and face.

Bucky didn't take me very seriously in the ring, either, and had to be constantly reminded to stay in a trot or to ignore the favored ferns that grew on the edges of the ring but had been picked clean in his pasture. He liked to step on my foot while I was putting his saddle on his back and then pretend he was asleep as I tried to push him off. Other times he would hold his breath and make his chest big while I tightened his girth, and then when we were in the ring, he would let all of the air out of his lungs so that on the next turn my saddle would slide off his back and onto the side of his belly, and I would end up hanging by one foot, trying to right myself long enough to pull my feet out of the stirrups and jump off safely before he made a break for the barn doors with me dragging behind in the dirt. But if he had been younger and I had been older, I like to think that we would have had the sort of girl-horse love that books are written about, that telepathic, transcendent love. I would have been covered in blue ribbons, he would have saved my life at least once, from a bear or a near-drowning or a pack of wolves, and I would have won a scholarship to one of those horsey colleges, where we would have gone together so we would never have to be apart. But time stood between us, and at the end of our fourth summer, Mary sent him and me out on a ride by ourselves and told me to say my good-byes, as Bucky was retiring to a pasture in town. I cried and proclaimed my devotion as he farted loudly enough to scare the birds off the branches all along the half-mile stretch of dirt road back to the barn.

Cosmos was the young draft horse. He was massive, with a shiny, wet-black coat and muscles that looked like the ones you see in a comic book. He had short legs, which made his center of gravity low and good for pulling things like logs and stone, and the big gentle eyes of a fawn, with thick black lashes. He was not the most cunning of animals; Mike needed only to put a fence across the path to keep him from going down to the creek. Cosmos would walk toward it, sigh, and turn around to plod back up the hill without it occurring to him that he could simply step off the path and walk around it. Cosmos never startled, never bit or nipped, and never seemed to get impatient or angry with any of us or the other horses. He was at the very bottom of the pecking order, or horse hierarchy, because he was the youngest and the least aggressive, which seemed to suit him just fine. After he was ridden or worked, he liked to roll in the dust with his short little legs in the air and scratch his back like a giant puppy, and he would sometimes seem to stare into the sky and ponder a cloud, or even close his eyes and let out big, snorty sighs.

Cosmos was the one that I took swimming in Paradise Pond, which was just over two miles away. Horses are natural swimmers, even the big ones. Vermont is muggy in the summertime, for which swimming is the best cure, especially if you are a child or an eighteen-hundred-pound horse with a black coat. And especially if you don't have cousins or a modest sister or a mother around to tell you not to take off your shirt. "This," said my uncle Mike, "is absolutely the last summer that you are going to be able to do that, Tupy." He had said the same thing the previous year and hadn't really been able to enforce it, though I had to admit that things were starting to look a little different up top and he was probably right. "I'm serious, people are going to start thinking I'm the funny uncle." I thought he meant funny ha-ha, which didn't seem to relate to the awkward development of my breasts, so I assumed he was doing us both the favor of changing the subject.

On these muggiest of days, you could jump in and feel the sweat and the damp, hot air, and the dirt, or most of it, leaving you in the water. You could even open your eyes underwater and see it, pulling away from you in a cloud. When you ride your horse into the water, the cloud around you is at first opaque and mixed in with the mud or sand from the bottom, and when the water around you is clear, you know that your horse's feet aren't touching the bottom anymore and that you are swimming. When you are riding a swimming horse, it's important to keep your whole body flat and near the surface, and to keep your feet up on his back because his legs are moving much more quickly than when they are on the ground, and if you were to get swept up in those legs, you could get kicked very hard and more than once. Cosmos's back was broad enough that you could stand on it and pretend that you were in the circus, and if you were light enough, dive from it into the water, and then swim back to him and pull yourself back on, over and over again. And after, when I rode him home, I would tie up his reins in the longer pieces of his mane so that they wouldn't slip over his head and trip him up, and I would stretch out on his back with my head on his rump and look up at the sky.

Peggy was the bitch. I always suspected that it was because she knew that Mike loved Butternut the most, but it could have just been the way she was. I avoided her most of the time, but I always felt like she was watching me, waiting for me to acknowledge her and her impressive status among the other horses. One summer, on Mike's birthday, my cousins and I brushed out her mane and tail and braided them. Into each of the braids' creases we stuck wildflowers that wilted almost immediately. Peggy seemed to like the attention at first, but soon enough she grew impatient. My cousins and sister backed away after her first bitchy little stomp, but I persisted. This had become an art project, and I was not about to let my work wander off. When she was completely covered, I paraded her into the ring and made her stand so that the group on the porch could admire her. "She looks like Carmen Fucking Miranda!" shouted Mike, lifting his beer bottle toward us. Peggy shifted her weight. Someone pitied us and gave us gentle applause, which she recognized as her cue to pull me back to the barn. She walked quickly and then broke into a trot, yanking me with her, a few of the daisies flying off her mane, and I heard some of the adults laugh, in a kind way.

Back in the barn I stood in front of her and unfastened her bridle. "You look pretty, Peggy, whether you know it or not," I said to her, smiling, with my eyes wide and my brows up, to show her that I was her friend. Her eyes narrowed and met mine, and she moved her nose slowly forward toward my chest. Assuming that she was going in for a nuzzle, I put my forehead against the bridge of her nose, which was when I felt her teeth close around my right nipple through my thin T-shirt. I opened my eyes and put my hand against her mouth and tried to pull away, but she had locked on now, with all four front teeth, top and bottom, and was looking straight at me. Her ears were falling back, in a sign of aggression, and she was beginning to turn her head slightly, pulling my chest up with her. My mouth opened but no sound came out. I dropped her bridle and her reins and pulled on her ears as hard as I could until she finally let go, just when I was about to give up, certain that the edges of her top teeth had met the ones on the bottom and that I had lost an important body part forever. Then I grabbed her tack, and I ran away from her and toward the house, my hand over my throbbing chest.

I didn't tell anyone what had happened because I wanted to keep riding, and by now every mother but mine had decided that Mike and Mary's horses were not safe to learn to ride on. It was weeks later, after my cousins had gone back to their cities, that I lifted up my T-shirt for my mother while she was in the tub, smoking, and showed her the bite. It was very swollen now, and surely infected. I hadn't been able to sleep on my stomach or even on that side; the skin had broken and then healed and then broken again, and now when I pushed against it, clear fluid came out. The bruise around it was as big as an apple, black and yellow and, in one spot, a sickly green. My mother sat up and put her cigarette down in the tin ashtray next to the tub. She saw it and pulled me, by the forearm, closer to her and, looking right at my nipple, said, "What happened to you?"

"Peggy bit me!" I cried out, tears coming out fast now. "Really hard."

She sat up straight, backing away slightly, and gave me a hard stare as she lifted her cigarette out of its tray and took a long, slow drag on it. "WHO," she said, adding a pause as though she were trying to stay calm, "the FUCK is Peggy?"

"The horse," I said.

"Mike's horse? The little red one?" she asked, looking a little relieved.

"Yes," I answered, "the little red one!"

She leaned back now, looking at my chest again, and sank back into the tub, holding her cigarette high. Her voice lowered and she shook her head as she said, "What a little bitch." I gave her a nod in agreement. Then she took another drag of her cigarette and looked at me again, and quietly told me to put alcohol on it every day and that if that didn't make the swelling go down, I was going to have to go to the doctor. She occasionally said that, but it never happened, which was fine with me.

A week later, my grandmother dropped off some clothes for me, and among the pile was a little bra. It was an almost useless thing, meant really just to flatten things out until I had something that needed supporting, but once I started wearing it, I also started wearing a shirt, because now when I wasn't, I looked like I was in my underwear. I had to admit that it was comfortable, especially when I was riding. Mike was right. That was the last summer.

HOW TO
make cream of
broccoli soup

Broccoli

BROCCOLI GROWS BEAUTIFULLY in Vermont. My mother grew huge amounts of it when I was small, and of cauliflower and cabbage. These plants grow like giant round roses, with their leaves stacked over one another in a circular pattern, their edible parts in the center, the outer leaves becoming tough and inedible as they grow outward and separate from the round core. My mother would tie up each cabbage to protect it from the sun and rain and bugs and to compress it and force it into a round shape, and when you untied it, you would find a hard, pale globe of thickly pressed leaves that you could not pull apart without splitting. Her broccoli and cauliflower, though, were left exposed to the elements, and because she did not take drastic measures against them, worms and other bugs fed on them.

I was impressed by the size of the broccoli and cabbages but more interested in the immediately edible things in my mother's garden. When we were small, my sister and I had eaten the peas and the carrots as soon as they appeared. We were worse than any family of rabbits or deer and could decimate whole rows of young vegetables in a single day. The insides of our shirts where we wiped the carrots clean would be covered in a fine, permanent dirt. By late summer, there would be more watery spaghetti squash and zucchini than anyone could want, so much that we would start to pick off the new blooms to keep them from turning into vegetables and pull back their long, reaching tendrils, wrapping them into bunches around our arms and leaving them in confused piles. There were cucumbers, which rotted quickly if you didn't find them first, and tall stalks of fennel used for pickling them. There were tomatoes, though never very many. Summer was short.

My sister and I were often hungry, because we were children and also because my mother wasn't the type to stock groceries in the house. On most days, there was rice and spaghetti in the cupboards and usually but not always a jar of peanut butter and some bread, and some butter and milk, but that was often it. There was always coffee and always beer, and absolutely always cigarettes, no matter what else we would run out of between Fridays, which was the day that my grandfather drove up our dirt road and handed my mother a check for seventy-five dollars, which was what we lived on. My mother tried to spend as little as possible on food, which she considered a low priority. She was not that interested in eating, and did not live on a daily schedule anchored by meals.

She was extremely thin and kept what appetite she must have had at bay with said coffee and cigarettes. She was always bringing it up, this burden of keeping us fed, and seemed to understand its importance well enough but looked to resources that did not seem, to us, reliable or consistent. "You two are like my baby birds," she would say, "always hungry, always needing me to find something to eat and stuff it down your throats."

I would think of the sparrows that nested in our eaves and of their new, blind babies, whom we would see stretching up their open beaks in unison, trampling one another in their desperate effort to be fed by their thin little mother, perched on the edge of the nest with a single worm, chewed up and ready to be split equally among them. This situation created an anxiety in me that lasts to this day. Even now, as an adult, I can only keep food in the house that requires cooking, because anything that can be eaten without preparation will disappear before I'm even aware that I've begun to open its packaging.

Our poverty drove my mother to resourcefulness. In the early spring, when her garden was still just dark and lumpy dirt, she hunted with spotty success for leeks and fiddleheads in the coldest, wettest, darkest corners of our woods, and we would go with her and whine as soon as our boots and socks had soaked through and become the same almost-frozen temperature as the thawing marsh. In the summer, she fished in the brooks and bogs, with just a simple rod and reel and no basket or tackle box, climbing upriver along the rocky bank in her tennis shorts and a bikini top and no shoes. I would follow her for a while, but as soon as I found a pool deep enough for swimming, I would stay there and wait for her because I didn't like the part where you have to kill the fish, which she did expertly but roughly by bashing its head against a rock. Usually she would come back with one or two small trout in her string bag, and I would get dressed and walk downriver to the trail that led back to our car, following her and poking at the silvery fishes hanging at her side. It was a full day for maybe one fish, or two fish, or sometimes none. She would clean and cook them in a cast-iron pan, and we would eat them, picking around the bones that she had broken during the bashing—they are the ones that don't easily come out when the guts and skeleton are removed—pulling out chunks of meat so fresh that it tasted not like fish at all but like the river with maybe just a hint of the Lucky Strike cigarettes that lived permanently in the string bag.

Most of my friends had fathers who hunted, and most of the boys and some of the girls I grew up with learned to shoot a gun before they were teenagers. I had friends whose families kept rabbits, which they butchered and ate on a daily basis, but none of these options were available to us for two reasons: First, my mother did not hunt, and second, I would not have eaten anything she killed if she had. As soon as I was old enough to understand what I was eating, I made two hard and fast rules: I would not eat anything that my mother had run over with the car (this was an option more than it should have been), and I would not eat anything that was cute, which rabbits most certainly were.

We may not have been the only family who ate what they killed or found or grew, but our methods, apparently, were an issue. My mother, despite her impressive skill set, was the subject of much criticism and very little acceptance within the small town where we lived. We were different, which, in a small town, is unforgivable. And—this is the hardest part—when the people in a small town, the ones who were there before you, know that you want to belong, to say that you are from that place, they recognize the power they have over you in denying you that, and they relish it and will point out the differences between you and them again and again and again. And they will do the same to your children, which is especially confusing. I could see from a very young age that my mother was strong and beautiful and talented. *Weren't these the things that people wanted to be?* I wondered.

When I returned to Vermont from California, in my second year of high school, my mother had moved into an old farmhouse in town, among a population of three hundred. Lisa Reynolds was the first friend I made. Her mother's house was across the street from my own, but it had also suffered a fire and was in a semi-permanent state of renovation. Once, when we were coming home from high school on the school bus—a forty-minute ride—and we stopped at Longley Covered Bridge to drop off Chris and Scott Longley, I saw the tail end of my mother's car parked by the path that went down to the river, under the bridge. I couldn't see her from where I was sitting, but Lisa could. "Looks like *Tess* is trying to *fish*," she said, as though it was the most foolish thing anyone had ever done on a riverbank.

Lisa's mother, Linda, and my mother were friends, and even though they were just as poor as we were, they treated us as though we were beneath them. We had all once gone—Lisa and I and our mothers—on a trip to a lake not far from where we lived. My mother had tossed a package of hot dogs and a bag of bread with four slices, including the two ends, and some ketchup into a paper bag for our lunch. When we were all in the car and Linda asked her what she had brought for lunch and my mother told her, her tone was exactly like Lisa's would be months later on the day at Longley Bridge, but louder and more cutting. "How the hell are you planning to cook a hot dog, *Tess*? You need to *cook* a hot dog!" I hated Linda from the backseat.

"I like mine raw," I said.

When we got to the lake, my mother took her Lucky Strike cigarettes out of her string bag and pulled her mini Bic lighter from inside the cigarette package, where it always lived. She walked straight to the picnic area with her paper bag in one hand,

and she found the small iron grill, which was on a stand near the wooden tables and metal trash cans. She pulled a few used paper plates from the trash can and picked up some branches from the ground, some of them with dried leaves still on them, and made a small pile right on top of the grill rack. She lit them with her lighter and then disappeared into the brush. I watched Linda's face, looking for signs of shame—desperately hoping that my mother would not come out of the trees, as she had once before on a similar forage for burnables, with someone else's used toilet paper in her hand—but Linda was a stone. At one point we could see some branches moving violently and heard some cracking. Again, Linda condemned her. She looked at the trees with her hands on her fat hips and shook her head, "Oh *Tess*, what the hell are you doing?" she asked nobody in particular. But even though I knew exactly what she was doing, I stayed quiet.

As the small sticks burned, they dropped as cinders through the grill and onto the ash pile left from someone else's charcoal briquettes. In less than ten minutes, there was a neat pile of them, red and glowing. My mother appeared out of the bushes just in time with some larger sticks, plus a few long, thin branches. She added the sticks to the fire and handed me the branches. I turned to Lisa with one of them and asked her if she was having a hot dog. She proudly reported that she was most certainly not and would be having half the grinder that her mother had bought for them at the store. Then my mother ripped open the bag of hot dogs with her teeth and grabbed one of them, stabbing it with the tip of my branch as though it needed to be made lifeless. She had broken off a branch in a way that left a piece of the bark trailing off at one end, which makes a nice sharp point for stabbing hot dogs. I knew the importance of taking branches off trees to cook your food with, because the wood is green and will not easily burn when you hold it in the fire, but this was a new opportunity for Linda, whose tone made it clear that she was beginning to lose a little steam now, to mock her. "You should have used a dry, dead branch, *Tess*, this place is a state park, you know, not your backyard." But by now we—*Tess* and I—were cooking our hot dogs, which required so much of our attention that we did not have time to hear her.

When mine looked done enough—I had burned it entirely, I remember—my mother took my stick from my hand and held it about a foot from the tip, where it was still quite hot. She then pulled a thick end piece of bread out of the bag, wrapped it around my charred hot dog, and, using it like an oven mitt, pulled the hot dog off the stick and handed it to me. I put some ketchup on it, too much because the glass bottle was hard to manage, and ate it in four bites. Then I ate my mother's hot dog, too, which was more expertly cooked, while she sat on the bench next to me, smoking a cigarette and drinking beer from a can. Lisa and Linda sat across from us, eating their sweaty grinder with its soggy bread and stinky old onions, and when they were finished, Lisa and I jumped into the water and left our mothers behind to gossip and bitch and drink their beers. We swam next to each other as she corrected my stroke and complained that my kick was too close to her face, until I was tired of her old onion breath hovering above the water and began to swim completely under the surface, away from her.

We were friends, Lisa and I, in much the same way our mothers were. She commented impatiently and harshly about almost everything I did and said my name as though it carried the same weight that my mother's did, as though we were beneath her somehow and not as clever. I knew that Lisa was smart, but I knew that I was smart, too. She knew more about boys; she had an older sister who was pregnant that summer and who talked to Lisa as though she were an adult. They would talk about the boys we knew, the ones who were just a little older than we were, calling them men—even Louis Snyder, whom I knew to dig extensive trails and highways in the sand pit behind his house and play with his toy trucks there, even though he was almost fifteen, and who I was sure was not a man at all but still a boy.

I was also sure we were still girls, even if we wouldn't be for too much longer. Lisa smoked cigarettes in the open and often carried a pack in plain sight, and could expertly blow a perfect series of thick white rings. And I had to admit that Lisa was superior to me in the only ways that counted, in my mind, that summer. She could dive like a bird from the highest, most precarious ledge at Second Hole into the smallest deep pool of water, in a place where I didn't even dare jump, much less dive, for fear that I would hit the rocks on either side of the pool. I wasn't even sure I could spot the right landing spot from the ledge, even though the water was so clear that you could see everything under it. And she, unlike me or any other girl or woman in town, could wear a pair of raggedy little cutoff shorts so beautifully that the rest of us felt, in her presence, like scabby little short-haired boys. She walked and stood and jumped as though she knew exactly what she looked like, while I wondered—no, obsessed—during that particular summer whether the eyes of the boys that I swam with saw a child or a woman or anything in between when they looked at me.

There were two ledges that met underwater at Second Hole, forming a tunnel that we would swim through, about four or five feet long. Every summer, we would look forward to diving down at one end and disappearing from the sight of anyone standing on the high rocks above us, and then emerging on the other side, seeming and feeling very brave. This summer when I tried it, I had not fit as easily and had been forced, in a panic, to squeeze my hips through the smallest part of the tunnel, holding my breath. I had come out of the water with scrapes along the tops of my legs, both of them bleeding, and much more profusely because of the cold water. I climbed back onto the rocks and wrapped myself in a towel, still shaken but not wanting anyone, especially Lisa, to see what had happened. That night I cut my jeans into shorts, while I was wearing them, and stood in front of the mirror. I was no Lisa Reynolds, but if I put my weight on one foot and my hand on my hip, I could almost imagine myself trying to buy cigarettes.

Because we learn from our mothers how to treat others, Lisa did not hide her disrespect for my mother from me. Even though she slept at our house whenever she felt like it, and ate our food, which was scarce; even though she sat on my bed one night in tears because she had not seen her mother for days and because of this had missed yet another appointment with the orthodontist. I knew she had already been wearing her braces for a year longer than she should have been. She had, herself, pulled out all the wires because they had become so loose and worn, and now all that remained were the little brackets, one on each tooth. I convinced her to let me pull them all off using the oddly perfect hole in the top of an old car key, just like a can opener, and I never once mentioned that I knew exactly where her mother was, that I had seen her car parked in front of the same bar every day for the last week, that the windshield had that many days' worth of dust on it, which was how long she had been with the man whose car she had left in, and that she was drinking, without stopping, with him. Lisa and I had this in common, these single mothers whose watchful eyes we had never thought we needed, until they turned away completely and left us terrified and alone.

After I took Lisa's braces off, we climbed out of my bedroom window onto the roof of the porch below, smoked cigarettes in our nightgowns, and talked about boys. If I had tried that summer to imagine what my future would look like, it would have been as much a mystery to me then as my own reflection in those cutoff shorts. This is what I understand now but could not have seen then: When you grow up in a home where nobody goes to work, where nobody is married, in a place where there are few jobs and few opportunities, you do not stay up late whispering about weddings and college and careers. You live in that moment, or maybe in the next; you do not make decisions that will impact a future that you do not let yourself imagine; you do not make a plan beyond your next pack of cigarettes.

But Lisa wasn't thinking about the similarities between us back when she saw my mother's car at Longley Bridge, when she was making every effort to point out the differences. My stop was the next one, and I got off the bus without making a plan to see her later, which I would usually have done. I walked through my front door and scanned the fridge, which smelled sour and hollow, and found a chunk of stale butter and some milk, which we always had because of coffee, and the broccoli that was left over from the garden, which had been mostly left to the fall. In the cupboard, I found a single bouillon cube and I began to make a roux, which would become a soup. The recipe was one that I had learned in Mrs. Grandshaw's home economics class, where traditional cooking and savvy coupon-cutting were the standard. When Mrs. G. announced that we would all be learning to cook a cream-based soup, I had recognized the ingredient list as manageable, even with our meager food supply, and I had memorized it. My mother came through the screen door with a bang just as I was adding the cut-up broccoli to the soup, dropped her bag on the floor, and put a tiny, speckled rainbow trout on the counter next to me. It was perhaps six inches long. It was dead but not cleaned.

"It's tiny. I should have gone somewhere else; there aren't any fish left under Longley Bridge," she announced as she pulled a can of beer from the fridge and opened it. I stared at the fish.

"How do you clean it," I asked, "when it's so small?"

She looked at me sideways, taking a drink from the can. "It doesn't make a difference, Heather, not at all." Another swig, and then, "You have no idea how to clean a fish, do you?"

She was smiling now, triumphant, really. She put her beer down and pulled a knife from the counter. "A daughter of mine should be able to clean a goddamned fish," she said loudly and gave me a thorough and disgusting recourse, through which she smoked two cigarettes. At the end of it, I was left with a tiny piece of fillet, which I gave mostly to the cats, and a pile of guts that I tossed onto her flower beds with her blessing. My mother and I had soup, which she complimented me on while finding a moment to roll her eyes over Mrs. Grandshaw. "Teaching you how to be a proper wife, is she?" she said, mockingly. But then she had more soup.

To make cream of broccoli soup, melt 2 tablespoons (30 g) unsalted butter in a large saucepan over low heat. Stir in 2 tablespoons (30 g) all-purpose flour. Add 2 cups (480 ml) milk, ½ cup (120 ml) at a time, stirring continually with a whisk. Add 2 cups (480 ml) vegetable or chicken stock, ½ cup (120 ml) at a time, until combined, then stir in 2 cups (455 g) finely chopped broccoli and a handful of minced fresh parsley. Finish with a pinch each of celery salt and white or cayenne pepper. Serve hot with good bread and beer, preferably an IPA.

HOW TO
make a very warm pair of pants

I WENT TO COLLEGE BECAUSE I HAD to go somewhere. My options were limited— my grades in high school had been less than stellar despite the best efforts of a few very supportive teachers and my clear knack for all things home ec. There wasn't any money. My father, whom I had little contact with, had decided that my mother's family could afford to send me easily, so he should not have to, and my grandfather had decided that doing so would spoil me and would continue my dependence on him at a time when he was beginning to realize that my mother would always need his help, which made him angry.

I learned this one day in June, right before I graduated from high school. I had come home from what was probably another day of swimming and smoking cigarettes at Second Hole just as his car was leaving our driveway, quickly. My mother was sitting in the kitchen. "Your grandfather was just here," she said, "and he told me that he's not going to be giving you any money for school, that he's changed his mind about helping you." It should have made me panic. If I had understood at that moment how hard it would be, I might have done just that. But I didn't know, so all I felt was relief. This meant that I could do what I wanted now, without his judgment or control, which was something that almost nobody in my mother's family had, but it also meant that I would be working while I was in school, and borrowing, and applying for more financial aid. I had chosen a local state college, perched on a high hill in a pretty little town, because I knew that I would be accepted (which I was, by the skin of my teeth) and because it was near enough to a ski resort where I felt confident I could get a job. It was like the town I had grown up in, but with a college. It seemed the logical choice.

The pressure to find work in a town without much going on had begun years earlier. I was paid for my first job when I was twelve, when I charged a truck full of rowdy college students from Montreal five dollars to show them the way to a swimming hole that they wouldn't have found without me. I rode in the back of the pickup with a few of them, and I could see they had little experience traveling this way because they were foolish enough to think that the bump formed by the wheel well was the best seat, when I knew it to only appear to be so and to actually be terribly bumpy, especially if you were starting to need the sort of bra that you didn't have.

As soon as I was old enough, I started working in a restaurant owned by a friend's parents, washing dishes and then waiting tables and eventually tending bar, all before I was legally allowed to set foot in a bar. I was a disorganized, unreliable employee. I had no car or telephone, no bank account, no watch. I was the waitress who wouldn't just forget about your ketchup or your straw but about you entirely. My tips were meager, but even if they had been more plentiful, I wouldn't have managed to save a cent. I spent whatever I earned on food—to finally be able to feed myself was thrilling—and on cigarettes, cheap makeup, and six-packs of beer (procured by the older brothers and sisters of friends).

When I found myself at the end of that final and rather social summer, and just days away from the day I was to move into the dorms, I had less than fifty dollars to my name. I put everything I owned into a black garbage bag and asked the older sister of a friend to drive me the sixty miles to my new home and school. My mother came along for the ride. Her license had been revoked for excessive and recurring speeding tickets, all of them written by the same town constable, who had a magnetic flashing light that he could mount on the roof of his unmarked car by just reaching out his window as he pulled out of his hiding place to chase down my mother. She contended that he was out to get her, and I didn't disagree, but the truth was that she had done nothing to avoid him or his speed trap, nor had she even once bothered to slow down. She and I sat in the financial aid office at Johnson State College, where we were helped through a series of simple applications and loan documents, and then I was allowed to move into my dorm room. My mother said good-bye, told me not to do anything stupid, and then was gone.

The thing that would make both college and holding down a job hard for me to manage was that I had difficulty with authority, having been raised with few limits and minimal supervision and by parents who did not have nine-to-five jobs, or even jobs. I had a similar approach to teachers as I did to bosses: I wasn't about to let anyone else decide what I did on a sunny afternoon, even if it was the week before finals. I skipped my very first college class—ethics, of all things—because I was invited to visit what was promised to me to be the finest swimming hole in the area (it was a total disappointment) by my resident assistant, who was supposed to be doing what he could to ensure my success as a freshman coed. When I showed up for that same class ten minutes early (that was an accident; I still didn't have a watch) two days later, I recognized a pretty girl from my dorm floor whom I liked immediately because I could tell that she didn't blow-dry her hair, either. (At the tail end of the eighties, this was as clear a political statement as any.) Plus, her sweater looked hand-knit. I took the seat next to her. "Were you here on Monday?" she said in a tone that made it seem OK to reply honestly that I had ditched class to go swimming, but that it had not been worthwhile. She gave me a raised eyebrow and smile, and a little nod, and then we were friends.

What quickly became apparent about Kerry and me was that while we liked exactly the same things—swimming in fresh water, bad weather, boys who were funny and who dressed like Grizzly Adams, wine of any color but especially pink, smoking Marlboro Reds while listening to sad music, knitting, and fries with gravy—we came from very different places. Kerry was from a lovely, woodsy town in Connecticut where everyone had jobs or had never needed them. She had been brought up along with a sister and a brother, both older, in a pretty house by a mother who took care of it and of them in a way that seemed effortless to me, and a father who worked as a stockbroker and came home before six every night. I had been hearing about all of this before Thanksgiving break of our sophomore year, when she offered me a ride to her house, where I would spend two nights before taking a train and then a subway to meet my own family in Brooklyn.

Family dinners, my own or anyone else's, always made me hold my breath. My mother came from a family that could not be called close. She and her three siblings had all grown up at separate boarding schools and maintained an intense competition with one another. There were only two times each year when my mother and her brothers and their children, and my sister and I, were together: when my uncles came and met their families in Vermont for two weeks each summer, and over Thanksgiving, when we were all in Brooklyn at my uncle's large house. Our days together in Vermont could be idyllic, full of swimming and tennis and berry-picking and long hikes in the woods. But something happened at dusk, and the dinners during these periods, held around a large, oval table in the kitchen in The Red House at the top of the mountain, were like poorly organized, sometimes violent tournaments.

My visiting uncles both worked in civil service, one in city government in New York City and the other for the World Bank, which required him to spend large chunks of time away from his family in Asia. Their discussions were about important political issues, and my mother's opinions were dismissed and belittled openly, regularly. All of us kids would listen as the tones among them grew less patient and more angry as the meal progressed. They would lay traps for one another, my uncles engaging another brother or their one sister in a dialogue, leading them into an argument that they could not win, questioning them in an increasingly patronizing tone, and finally delivering a single blow that left the defending party angry and hurt. But when their prey reacted angrily, when my mother or a brother tried to stand up for themselves, their older brothers would switch instantly to an expression of concern and dismay, assuring everyone that they had not done anything wrong, that their target was just sensitive, overreacting, unstable. It could slowly drive a person crazy.

We, the younger generation, would slip away quietly and meet again upstairs, where we would listen to the final rounds, until my uncle Mike, the youngest brother, would leave with a slam of the screen door, and my mother would call to us from the stairway, angry and without patience, and demand that we get in the car immediately, that it was time to go. We would walk slowly up the huge, sloping lawn in the dark, with millions of stars and sometimes the moon over our heads. One night my mother was especially angry and had walked out with her still half-full glass of wine. "Mom, you can't drive with that," I said. "You're right," she answered, and with a single motion of her arm, she splashed the contents of the glass through the open window of my uncle Halsey's car, onto its steering wheel and dashboard. I felt proud of her, at that moment, because it hurt to see the way she was treated by them, and I wanted so much for her to able to beat them, just once.

So I dreaded family gatherings, and dreaded even more the rides home afterward with my mother, driving recklessly, muttering and smoking. My father once told me that my mother talked to herself, out loud, and that this made him very nervous when they were married. I explained to him that she wasn't talking to people who she believed were there, that she was merely continuing one of the many arguments she had with her family members, and that it didn't matter whether they were in the room or not. I wonder still if it ever occurred to my uncles that the sport of belittling her could mean such a dangerous ride home for my sister and me. My cousins and I, as much as we loved one another and hated the way our parents treated each other, modeled their competitive behavior, staging mock Olympic games, short-sheeting each other's beds, and putting each other's underpants in the freezer. It was usually the boys against the girls, just like at the dinner table. Still, these were games, and we loved and protected one another in the way that siblings would. Even though our behavior toward one another was never mean-spirited, I would become furious if I felt that I was being disrespected or mistreated, and I would try to stand up for myself in the way that I wanted my mother to stand up for herself against her brothers.

I think I expected dinner at the Canfields' house to be the same because I vaguely recognized in Kerry's descriptions of her home life the same trappings of intellectual, WASP-y America that my family clung to. Or maybe I couldn't imagine that a family like Kerry's really existed, with nobody coming to the table already angry, fighting for position.

We were greeted at the door by Kerry's sister, Kim, and mother, Virginia. Kim was just a year older than Kerry and was attending Dartmouth. She was soft-spoken, sweet, and clearly brilliant. There were no self-celebrating family photographs hanging on the walls of their gray clapboard house, just small and simple paintings that were, I knew, very good and also mismatched enough that I could assume that they were all of places or by people that mattered to the family. They welcomed me with a polite warmth and expressed interest in my extremely unremarkable and half-assed pursuit of a college degree in a way that made me wonder whether being accepted into a small state college (again, by the skin of my teeth), where I was pulling straight Cs, was actually a much bigger deal than I thought.

Kerry's father, David, came home minutes after we got there and walked straight into a room that seemed dedicated to both cocktails and memorabilia related to what looked like an idyllic country club and its golf courses. There was a small television hidden in a cabinet that would never, ever, in the dozens of visits to come, be turned on in my presence unless there was an important golf game on or a movie night had been announced. Kerry showed me the large room that she and her sister shared while her parents had drinks in thick glasses with lots of ice cubes. Dinner was mostly ready and had been left warming before any of us had walked through the door. I was standing with Kerry in the small half bath across from the back door when her older brother, Chris, came home from a long run. He was ridiculously handsome. His jaw looked as though it had been carved from a giant block of cold butter and his eyes were bright and blue. His excitement in seeing Kerry pulled him right into the bathroom with us. I had never seen a brother show such clear love and admiration for his own sister. He smiled the whole time he spoke to us, his perfect white teeth gleaming, with a loud, confident voice and a laugh that sort of reminded me of the old men from *The Muppet Show*, except that the old men from *The Muppet Show* were not sexy, nor were they wearing very tight, stretchy, sweat-soaked long-sleeve tees in a deep navy blue that set off their ruddy cheeks and blue eyes. Chris paused between every word, confident that we would wait patiently for the next, stretching out his thoughts carefully. He was mesmerizing. He looked at Kerry with an obvious, protective pride. He gave me a polite but slightly suspicious glance.

Chris left us for the shower and appeared again just before we all sat down, dressed as though he was going to a school dance. Dinnertime conversation began with updates on neighbors, mostly glowing and only ever-so-slightly gossipy. News in my hometown was usually about which couple had most recently split or who had driven their car straight into the mud-room of the Thirsty Boot Saloon after accidentally putting it into first gear while trying to back out of the parking lot. News in Ridgefield, at least in this stage of the Canfields' family life, was about who had been accepted into which prestigious school, and how Kerry's tight group of high school friends, who had been adopted into their family the way I would eventually be, were faring at their respective colleges. Mr. Canfield was funny and clearly loved his children, and I adored him.

Kim asked me about where I had grown up, and I kept things sort of vague. Kerry had undoubtedly filled in her family on my unconventional situation, on the fact that I was financing my own education through a last-minute flurry of student loans and a patchwork of part-time jobs and on how I lacked the life skills or maturity to be doing it with much success or grace. Virginia asked me more questions about my parents than I could answer without making them seem negligent, but this had always been the problem with talking about my mother and father. I suddenly felt the need to paint a picture of my family that was appealing, perhaps rugged and rural, yes, but uniquely classy. My mind went quickly to the cover of the October L.L. Bean catalog sitting in the Canfields' foyer. I tried to steer the conversation toward my mother's admirable skills and talents at surviving in a remote part of Vermont with few resources. Somehow this led to Chris asking me a question that I wasn't expecting. "And does your family usually hunt and dress its own Thanksgiving turkey?" Clearly I had gone too far in painting a picture of my mother as a survivalist. The only wild game that she ever killed was whatever was unlucky enough to find itself in the path of her speeding Honda. My answer came too fast, with little thought to how it would sound. "No, we go to my uncle's house in Brooklyn," I said. "But if we were at home we wouldn't be able to get a turkey anyway, because they are really hard to hunt."

Chris's eyebrows shot up. "And why, pray tell, is that?" he asked, genuinely interested.

If I had thought for a moment before I had spoken, if I had

said the words to myself, the ones that I had heard so many times that I had never questioned them, I would have realized how ridiculous they would sound when uttered in Ridgefield, Connecticut. But, instead, I spoke. "Because," I said, "they can throw their voices." Chris dropped his fork and leaned back in his chair, as his eyebrows went up at least two inches, a smile slowly spreading across his face. "Do they?" he said, smugly. Kerry and her mother bit their bottom lips and lifted their eyes toward me. Kim scolded Chris protectively, using only one eyebrow, which won my heart, but it was David who leaned forward and told me, "Go on."

I told the Canfields as much as I knew about wild turkeys, about how Benjamin Franklin had wanted a turkey to be on the nation's official seal, instead of the bald eagle, because he believed the turkey to possess the same characteristics as the wily, outgunned revolutionary and the bald eagle to be a scavenger and a thief that stole its prey from the hardworking raptors after they were tired from a successful hunt. He believed that the bald eagle represented the imperialist, not the free man. I told them about the turkey that had been served at a town hall dinner in northern Vermont, when I was very small, that was meant to help fund a free dental clinic, and how the bird had been shot at by so many hunters that three people had broken teeth on the buckshot still in its meat, themselves now requiring a dentist. I didn't tell them about the turkey that my mother had hit, or how she had had to pry it out of the broken grill of her car and then had run over it again, this time on purpose, an act that would have seemed more humane had she not been doing almost sixty on a narrow dirt road in the first place.

What was remarkable about the Canfields, on that evening, was that they listened to me. I had never sat like this at a table, surrounded by a family interested in what I had to say, and was torn between my luck at having found them and my jealousy at not having it for my own. I was beginning to picture the rest of my stay with them, which I had hoped would be much more of this, being listened to and fed delicious food surrounded by nice people, until Chris announced that he was doing a little landscaping work for the parents of a friend the next day and that he wanted to take Kerry and me along to help. Kerry agreed because she was his sister and because she was always eager to earn a little money during breaks and the summer, and I didn't feel like I could say no, as a guest, but immediately felt the heat in my face that was a symptom of my issues with authority, and instinctively I tried to find a way out. I reminded Kerry that we had a friend coming over the next day, a dorm mate who lived on Long Island, also on her way home for Thanksgiving. She would arrive in the early morning. "Perfect," said Chris, "I'll have three helpers." He got up from the table without making eye contact with me and went out for the evening. I wondered what sort of girl Chris Canfield would spend an evening with. Probably one who had been accepted at a good college and did not have a mother who ran over turkeys, at least not on purpose.

Chris woke us up far too early. Meredith had been dropped off even earlier. She had grown up on Long Island and had worked at a clothing store in Manhattan during high school, and every piece of clothing she owned had a title that included the designer's name and a description, and when she referred to each of them, you could hear the capital letters in their titles. I found it strange that she didn't seem to notice how little thought the rest of us put into our wardrobes. She once joined us for a quick dip in the river in a Hand-Block-Printed Putumayo Sarong, a fluorescent orange Adrienne Vittadini Gold Ring Tankini, and pair of Ralph Lauren Cross-Strap Sandals. Kerry was wearing a Pair of Shorts That Had Once Been a Pair of Pants, and I was in a swimsuit that had small rips in its sides from where I had stuffed beer bottles into it to sneak into the movies. Swimsuits were pretty much my only undergarment for six months out of the year in those days.

When we filled Meredith in on Chris's plans she looked dubious, but when she saw Chris, now dressed in sturdy work clothes that made him look exactly like the sad, handsome, young, widowed farmer to whom more than a page had been devoted in her last J. Peterman catalog, she perked up. She pushed past me waving a hand. "I just need to change quickly!"

The three of us rode together with Chris on the long bench seat of his vintage red pickup truck. His outfit and accoutrements, which included an old-fashioned push mower, made me wonder whether this was really his true calling, or whether he was like some of the people who moved to our town in Vermont, driven by aesthetic and romantic notions of manual labor, only to move on to something more academic once the tips of their fingers started to split open. He was clearly smart and capable and could be doing anything with his post-college self, so why was he living at home and cleaning up the yards of wealthy neighbors? Whatever romantic notions he had, I decided I wasn't on board. Who was he to tell me to work in the dirt all day, just because I was his sister's friend? Was this any way to treat a guest?

As we drove through that sleepy, wooded suburb, past the beautiful houses with three cars each, I felt like an imposter, unsuccessful in my attempt to pass for someone who belonged there, my real identity having been ferreted out by Chris and by Meredith, who now ignored me and listened to each other. I was sure that they thought of me as a silly hick, especially now that I was sitting next to Meredith, who was dressed in her Patagonia Blueberry Fleece Tights, Mephisto Leather Walking Shoes, and Banana Republic Slightly Sheer Ecru V-Neck Tee. I was wearing the same thing I had been wearing the day before. In my defense, nobody told me to pack for dinner *and* landscaping. I had a single dress with me for Thanksgiving dinner, and I would have worn it to dinner the night before, but it was on loan from Kerry, who had inherited it from her sister.

As I became more resistant to the idea of getting out of the truck, Meredith chattered nonstop about every important place and person she and Chris might both know, throwing her head back and laughing as though she had shared oh-so-many bohemian adventures with so-and-so, more than she could recount, really, all of them so special, in Greenwich Village and SoHo and at this and that club. It was tempting to remind her that she was barely nineteen. I was annoyed. Kerry was quiet, watching her neighborhood go by. We pulled up in front of a pretty house with more than its fair share of lawn and rock gardens. Meredith jumped out and took possession of the push mower, gave Chris a cute smile, and began her solo, morning-long catwalk back and forth across the lawn. This left Kerry and me to the weeds. I was led to a small bushy area by the side of the house, while Kerry was trusted with an actual tool. As soon as I was alone, I began to dig. It had not been as cold in Connecticut as it was already in Vermont, so I found what I was looking for quickly: three very long, very pink earthworms. I carried them back to the cab of the truck and climbed into it without anybody knowing. I lay down on the bench seat and, working humanely, tied each of the worms into a double knot around the steering wheel. Then I slipped out of the truck and back to my spot in the weeds. We were there for more than an hour, which was enough time to make me worry about the well-being of my worms. Finally, Chris told us that it was time to go, and we gathered our things and walked back to the truck. Meredith scooted ahead of me and slid in through the driver's seat, ensuring her spot next to Chris. She didn't see them right away. I slid in next to her, and Kerry and Chris got in last. One of the worms had wriggled free; I could see him next to the gas pedal, but out of the way of Chris's boots. The other two had made pretty good strides toward freedom; one of them was almost completely untied and stretching one of its ends upward toward Chris's chin. The other, which I had placed at two o'clock, caught Chris's attention just before his hand hit the wheel. His palm opened flat and his fingers stayed splayed, his jaw dropped, and his mouth opened not in horror, but in a state of speechlessness. Meredith let out a horrified gasp. "*That*," she said, speaking to me as though I were a child, "is disgusting." Kerry looked at me, shocked and clearly annoyed. "Heather!" she said, "Why would you do that?" as Chris untangled the two worms and then opened his door to return them.

We rode home in silence. When we pulled into the driveway, Chris jumped out without saying a word, and Meredith and Kerry followed. I reached down to the floor of the driver's side, scooped up the third, hidden worm, and rolled him out onto the thick, perfectly trimmed and watered Canfield lawn. This was an excellent spot for a worm, I was certain of that. I said my soft apologies to him and let him go.

Chris never offered me a job again. I continued to take seasonal work at horse barns and resorts, teaching riding or skiing, childhood skills that I was surprised to find out were marketable. I was no expert at either but good enough to teach beginners. Of

course, those jobs—and bosses—only lasted a few months by definition. Authority made me anxious, it made me feel small and powerless, and in that state I would act out compulsively, irresponsibly. Eventually I realized that I was better off working for myself.

Seeing people like Meredith, who would pay so much money for a pair of stretchy fleece tights, inspired me to begin making warm clothing—fleece was the hottest thing in fabrics at that time—to sell to my classmates. In the middle of my sophomore year, I moved out of the dorms and into a house in town, where I kept a sewing machine in the front hall of the apartment I shared with three other girls, which likely annoyed them to no end. I used this machine to make pairs of warm fleece tights for my friends and classmates, using a simple formula to create a pattern that would fit them perfectly. We lived in warm layers like these, in our poorly insulated rented apartments located in old hotel buildings

To make a pattern for fleece tights, gather these measurements: your waist, hip, and ankle circumference, and your outseam (or length from waist to ankle bone). ● Tape together 2 pieces newspaper so length is as long as you want leggings to be plus a few inches, and width is as long as your arm. Starting from a top corner a few inches from side edge of paper, with a thick, black marker, draw a line parallel to long edge of your paper that measures the length from your waist to ankle bone, plus 2" (5 cm). At one end of line, draw a perpendicular line as long as your waist divided by four, plus 1" (2.5 cm). Label that line "waist." 9" (23 cm) below that line, draw a parallel line as long as your hip measurement, divided by four, plus 1" (2.5 cm). Label this line "hip." Draw a line parallel to the hip and waist at the bottom end of paper that is your ankle circumference divided by four, plus 1" (2.5 cm). Label this line "hem." Connect ends of hip and waist lines with a curve, as shown, and connect end of hip line and ankle line with a straight line. Using paper scissors, cut out your custom pattern. ● To make the tights, fold in the ends of a 2-yard (2 m) piece of double velour 4-way stretch fleece with right sides together so both of its selvedge edges meet in center, creating two folded edges. Place your pattern on one side, with its long straight "outseam" edge along fold, and trace using a refillable chalk pencil. Flip pattern over, and repeat on other side, with pattern's outseam along opposite folded edge. Cut out the two leg pieces, leaving folded edge uncut. With fabric still folded, right sides facing, sew each pant leg closed by stitching along inseam using a ½" (12 mm) seam allowance and a medium-width zigzag stitch, back-tacking at start and finish. Repeat with other folded leg piece. Turn one leg right side out and put it inside other leg, with inseams matched up. Sew crotch seam together with a ½" (12 mm) seam allowance and a medium-length zigzag stitch, back-tacking at start and finish. Unfold legs and turn both legs wrong side out. Fold waist edge over 1" (2.5 cm) and sew down, capturing its raw edge with a medium-width, short-length zigzag stitch, creating a tunnel and leaving a 2" (5 cm) opening in center front for elastic. Using a seam ripper, gently pull both ends of thread on both sides of this opening to wrong side, and tie them to each other to finish seam invisibly. Cut a piece of ¾" (2 cm) waistband elastic so it equals your waist measurement plus ½" (12 mm). Attach a large safety pin or bodkin to one end and thread through waistband tunnel. Overlap the two ends and stitch them together using a medium-width, medium-length zigzag stitch. Hand-sew waist opening closed.

and rambling farmhouses. It was a good little income for me and would be the thing that I turned to, much later, as a career.

The Canfields, on the other hand, became the one constant in my life. I would not have been able to stay in college as long as I did without them, not emotionally, not practically, not financially. They remain dear to me to this day, more than twenty years after that first dinner. When Kerry's father was dying, I was living in California, and I flew back to Connecticut to see if I could help. Kerry's bedroom was the same as it always had been, more familiar to me now than any home I had ever shared with either of my parents. On her dresser sat a familiar Beatrix Potter Peter Rabbit address book. I opened it to the page that held my name and saw, in a long list that covered the page and the one next to it, plus every small margin, each of the more than twenty addresses where I had lived over the previous decade, even the ones that had lasted only a few months, all of them except the most recent crossed out.

Chris and I eventually became good friends, too. He stayed handsome and idealistic and married a beautiful girl who was raised more like me than like him, and they live in a tiny New Hampshire town with their two intelligent, beautiful, free-spirited girls. When I got married, at the age of thirty-seven, I asked Chris to officiate. He still had that lovely voice and that confident presence. I explained my reasons to TC and assured him that Chris would do a great job, that he had once been a teacher so we could count on his ability to hold the attention of our guests. TC agreed, and even told me that his parents approved, which surprised me given their dedication to the Catholic Church. Chris did not disappoint. He delivered a funny, personal speech and made me feel, along with his parents and Kim and Kerry, that I was surrounded by people who had always known me, and always loved me, even before I was the person that I was always meaning to be.

A year after my wedding, I asked TC what he wanted to do for our first anniversary. "I think we should call Chris," he said, "and just check in. You know, tell him how things are going and ask if he has any words of wisdom or advice. It's what my brother and his wife do with the minister who married them, once a year, on their anniversary."

"But," I said, "Chris isn't our minister."

"Yes, but he used to be a preacher, so he'll be fine with it," TC responded.

I gave TC a look that prompted him to add, "You told me that he used to be a preacher!"

"No," I told him, "I said that he used to be a *teacher.*"

I asked TC not to share this revelation with his mother. There wasn't any way for me to explain to her, or even to TC, that if I had to bow to anyone's authority on my wedding day in order to get the job done, I wanted it to be Chris Canfield's.

HOW TO
run away

I MOVED IN WITH MATTHEW AT THE beginning of my fourth year of college. He was from Shelburne, Vermont, and had also been brought up by a single mother, which is different for a boy than for a girl but also the same. He was a few years older than I was. Instead of going to college immediately after high school, he had followed the Grateful Dead around the country for two years and become a remarkably successful businessman, procuring and selling pot to fellow travelers and, when he did finally go to college, to students.

We lived in a very small, very sweet house together in Stowe, forty minutes or so from Johnson State and maybe twenty minutes from the restaurant where I waitressed. It was also near the ski area where Matthew went almost every day of the season, with his puffy red eyes and his snowboard. I had dated other boys at Johnson but nobody whose upbringing was even slightly similar to mine. Matthew was more like the boys that I had gone to high school with, proud of their guns and of their cars and of their ability to force their cars into fast, tight circles in empty parking lots and snowy fields. Matthew owned several guns, including deer rifles and handguns, and a large, amber-colored bong with a huge NRA sticker on it. Matthew had been happy and funny in the beginning, convinced that he was moving toward good things, but after we had lived together for a few months, I could see that he was becoming less satisfied with me and was more frequently falling into dark moods that, when fueled with alcohol, would lead to destructive behavior: a fist through a window followed by the roar of his car on the gravel, tearing out of our driveway. This was comfortable, familiar ground for me. When he punched a wall and broke through the drywall, it was my mother who gave him step-by-step instructions on how to make the necessary repairs.

He was a student when we started dating, but then he had needed to go to Mexico for a few months because some of his business partners were being arrested, and when he came back, he did not re-enroll. Now he was growing a large number of pot plants in our basement with the help of photovoltaic lights, which seemed to require a lot of his time.

I had been a student, too, but by the time the spring semester began, I was working full-time as a very bad waitress instead. I had convinced myself that school was not as important as Matthew and that we would be happier—*he* would be happier—if we had more money and a nice car that ran well and had four-wheel drive. We shared a sense of futility where college was concerned, deep down believing, though we never said it, that it was for spoiled rich kids and could not give us what we needed to survive the lives that we were building for ourselves. "I think your best bet," he said to me one night right before I left school, "would be to find a small company that might be big someday, and to get in on the ground floor, doing something maybe in the office, where they need a pretty girl, and then stick it out. I could totally see you," he said, "wearing high heels."

Leaving school meant no longer seeing even my closest friends at Johnson, which was more of a surprise to me than it should have been. They moved on without me, getting through their last years and shifting their focus to what they would do next, after school, when they went home to Connecticut or New York. But that was the thing with Matthew and me: We were home, we had never left, we had nowhere to go back to.

One night, after a waitressing shift riddled with mistakes, the owner of the restaurant where I worked told me that I was fired. I had just purchased four new logo-emblazoned turquoise polo shirts—a requirement of the job—and this was the first thing I thought of when I got the news. Later, I would boast that I had told the owner that I wanted him to buy back the shirts and that if he didn't, I would paint swastikas on them and wear them around town, and that he had given me my money back. This was all true except that I was sobbing when I did it, a detail I didn't mention back then. I had gotten a ride into work that night because my old, rusted, completely illegal car had finally died, so I had to call Matthew and wait outside, by the restaurant's back door and Dumpster, for him to pick me up.

I waited for almost an hour, and when he did come, he was drunk. We went to a restaurant that was open late, and I used the thirty dollars from the polo shirts to pay for Matthew's dinner. By this time, Matthew was behaving as though allowing me to be by his side was an honor that I did not deserve and that buying his meals was the least I could do to show my appreciation. Things had been this way long enough that I had begun to believe him. He was silent on the way home, and when we reached the driveway to our house, he sped up and drove past it.

The gravel roads were icy and the meadows had at least two feet of snow, at least half of it fresh. He yanked the steering wheel to the right and suddenly we weren't on the road anymore but in a pasture, and the car was spinning, in loose control, and then his headlights were off and it was just the moonlight over us as we spun, silently, in fast circles through the thick snow. "You are going too fast," I said, thinking then that the ride was supposed to be fun.

"Am I scaring you, Heather?" he asked. "Are you afraid, Heather?" he continued, his voice calm, slick, and patronizing, and then loud. "Are you AFRAID?" he asked again.

"Yes," I said. "You are going to hit a goddamned tree; slow the fuck down!" He didn't stop, though, not until I was crying and holding on to the door handle with both hands, and then he pulled the car back onto the road and leaned over me, pushed open my door, and shoved me out into the snow. "I'm fucking out of here!" I heard him yell as he sped off with the door still open. I walked home, in the moonlight, and found him there, tearing our little house apart, piece by piece. I hated Matthew with all of my heart at that moment, when I found him in the rubble of our living room, not gone at all, like he had promised. This, after all, is why boys in the country drive in fast circles, it's why they throw drunk punches and say they will leave but never do. It's because they have no place to go.

A few days later I sat in my small living room. I had no job, I was no longer in school, and—I was finally starting to see— I had no future with Matthew. The phone rang; it was his mother. I told her what had happened, that Matthew had torn apart our house, broken windows and punched walls, and that he had decided that I was almost worthless. "His father did that once," she said, "and he told me that he was leaving me, but he didn't go. I looked back many times, over the years that followed, and wished he had gone, and not come back."

Without a job, I could not pay rent, and so I moved out of that small, sweet house and in with my mother, who was living in a house that she was caretaking, and got a job as a bartender at a restaurant on the other side of the mountain, in Jeffersonville. On my first day off, I borrowed her car and drove to the bookstore in Burlington and looked through books about internships. I thought that maybe I could be a teacher, and I loved to be outdoors, so I selected an internship in environmental education in Mendocino, California. I copied down the phone number and address onto a scrap of paper and returned the book to its shelf. I saved a little bit of money, not very much, and flew, over Christmas, to California to see my father and my sister. I had applied for the internship and had an interview with its director in Berkeley. My sister drove me to the meeting from Santa Cruz, and we talked about how nice it would be to live on the same coast. Her life seemed so clean, so stable to me. She had stopped coming to Vermont in the summers, and while she never said it, I could tell that she thought of it as nothing but a place full of dead-end roads and sad, poor people who drank too much. I knew that she was wrong, but I also knew that there was nothing there for me, at least not now.

I met the director of the environmental education program in a busy bakery in Berkeley, surrounded by earthy-looking people. Penny was tiny, with a sweet face and a very small, almost high, voice. We talked about being outside, about my having grown up outdoors, and about why I thought it was important that kids feel comfortable in nature, if not close to it. I told her about the beaver pond and about the frogs that I had caught and saved. "You are certainly an environmentalist," she said. Then she leaned in to ask me a final, logistical question. "This job is an internship. We will give you a place to live in one of our on-site cabins, but you'll only be paid seventy-five dollars a week. Are you sure you'll be able to get by on that?"

"Yes," I said, "I believe I will."

I saved up as much as I could during the rest of the winter, which wasn't very much, and then bought a train ticket from Waterbury, Vermont, to Los Angeles, California, for $312. The night before I left, Matthew and Elaine, a good friend, one of the few who were still in Vermont, came to say good-bye. My mother was angry at me all the time now because I had borrowed her car too many times or because I was leaving or because she didn't know when I was coming back. Once, when Penny called our house to talk to me about housing, my mother had asked her, "How long will Heather be in California?" On the night before I left, after drinking five beers, she turned to me, with Matthew and Elaine looking on, and said, "You've been treating my home like a hotel, you spoiled little brat. Now it's time to check out." And then she stumbled up to bed. I almost left without saying good-bye, but at the last minute she came down the crooked little stairway and wrapped her long, thin arms around me, and held me, and told me not to do anything stupid. And then I drove away from her house in Elaine's car, with Matthew following behind us. She stood in the window, and I could see that she was crying.

I rode a bus to Springfield, Massachusetts, and boarded a train that took me to Ohio. From there I went to Idaho, then Jackson Hole, Wyoming, where I spent a few days with friends. Then I caught a ride with other friends to Salt Lake City, where I boarded another train to Los Angeles, traveling south into the high desert, away from the Rocky Mountains. It was warm enough on the second night to walk between the train's passenger cars to the luggage cars, which had big sliding windows that could be pushed open, and lean out into the current of desert air and see the stars. I stayed up all night, leaning against a pile of suitcases, smoking cigarettes, and looking at the sky, watching the moon rise and then disappear again.

My sister and her husband met me in Los Angeles the next morning and drove me all the way, a full ten hours, to Mendocino. I hadn't realized how far it was, having mistakenly assumed that since both towns were in the same state that the distance between them couldn't be more than a few hours. We had lunch in Mendocino, a beautiful town that surprised me because it felt and looked like it could be in coastal Maine or Massachusetts. Then we drove down an endless, narrow gravel road into the bit of old-growth redwood that still remained until we reached a dark little grove, under which sat my tiny cabin. Around one side wrapped a small, dark stream, thick and quiet, surrounded by deep green moss and high ferns. It felt like a forgotten forest, an ancient Jurassic place, with trees so high and dense that even though it was midafternoon it felt like evening. Penny met me on the road, brought me into the dining hall, and introduced me to the naturalists and then the kitchen staff. I walked back to my cabin and said good-bye to my sister, who looked worried to be leaving me there. I told her that I would buy a car soon—how I thought I would do this, on seventy-five dollars a week, I do not know—and visit her often, and then I was alone, standing in what felt like a new world, suddenly aware that nobody waiting for me in the dining hall knew anything about me.

The Mendocino Woodlands, a place that I had picked—no, stolen—randomly from a thick book that I had pulled off a shelf in a bookstore, was a lucky landing spot. It happened to be a place where community, above all else, was valued, where the staff was nurturing, supportive, and exceedingly nonjudgmental. The place itself was bare-bones, beautiful, and rustic; the woods were dark and wet and always green, and the paths through them were almost hidden, and lonely and peaceful. It was as much of a resting place as I could have hoped for. I tried to make fires at night in my little stone fireplace, but its chimney had been so cold and so wet for so long that it was nearly impossible. Still, it wasn't as cold as what I had known before, and eventually I would break the anxious habit of always wanting to start a fire and keep it going, and I would learn to seek out spots in the sun, which is what the other naturalists, the ones who had grown up in California, always did. We would sit for hours in the meadows, on our days off, and talk about all the things that we wanted to do, with each other, with our lives, with our futures.

My job was to introduce children to nature in a way that fostered wonder, respect, and stewardship. Each week a new batch of them arrived in a school bus, and we would bring them out into the meadow, where there was sun, and introduce ourselves and this place to them. On my third or fourth week at the Woodlands, we welcomed a group of sixth graders from a public school in the Napa Valley, many of them children of farm workers. We had been told that many of these kids would leave high school to work in the fields, that most did not speak English at home, that their communities were full of drugs, even gangs. We would always begin introductions by acting out a skit for them, each of us taking the role of an animal or an inanimate object, and teaching them the basic rules that would govern our community for the coming week. I was a "rock" that week, which meant that I would be the thing that the "child" who was running through camp would trip over. I still had the large laminated placard with the word "ROCK" around my neck when the skit had ended and we were introducing ourselves to our students.

"My name," I said, "is Rock."

"No, it isn't!" said one little girl.

"Yes, it is, at least for this week," I said. "And since we've only just met, you can't really say it isn't my name, can you? And if there is anyone here who would like to be someone new this week, someone who doesn't get into trouble, say, even though maybe they do at home, this is your chance, because I've never met you, and neither has anyone else here. Whoever you tell me you are, I will believe you."

A thin boy, in clothes that had clearly belonged to somebody else before they had been his, stepped forward and held up his hand. "OK, then," he said, turning to his classmates and his teachers and throwing up both of his arms with beaming pride. "My name is *Spiderman!*" And then his classmates and his teachers, and me, and all of my new friends, we clapped and shouted for him.

HOW TO
fend off a bear

WHEN I TOLD MY SISTER, OVER THE phone, that I was moving in with Mick, she didn't even try to hide her disappointment.

She had been thrilled when I moved to California and generally happy when I ended up in Mendocino, which was just four hours up the coast from Scotts Valley, where she now lived with her husband in a tidy suburban house surrounded by excellent schools and pretty vistas and good jobs. But she had always been worried about whether or not I might meet a nice man there and start a family, which was her singular focus.

In Mendocino, I worked seasonally as a naturalist and wilderness guide and, for a time, at a horse barn. I traveled between jobs anywhere I liked, with whomever I wanted, on the cheap. My sister was getting impatient with my lifestyle because it didn't seem to be leading to settling down and because it was clear that the men I was meeting and dating were prone to wandering, trying to avoid responsibility and competitive career fields. Once, I called her after a date. "What does he do?" she asked, carefully.

"He's a surfer," was my reply, which was met with a long silence.

"I meant, as a *job*."

"Oh, well, he bartends sometimes and waits tables. He wants to keep his days free for, you know, surfing."

"Why don't you just date an alcoholic?" she said. "They are free most nights."

There were things about Mick that she liked, like the fact that he had a job—he was a contractor—and a nice family. There were also things about Mick that she didn't like, such as the fact that he was ten years older than I was, that he lived in Arcata, which meant that I would be seven hours away instead of four, and most of all, that he lived in a teepee.

Mick was a woodworker and a builder, specializing in craftsman-style design. He pulled down old barns and water towers and built new homes and structures from them, beautiful structures that made me believe, along with his earnest demeanor and seemingly impressive work ethic—he went to work every morning at five—that one day we would live in a sound and lovely house and that this would be my home and my life.

When I told my sister that I had planned to move in with him, her response was, "Are you going to get married?"

"I'm not really sure," I said, because I wasn't.

"I'll give you three years," she said, "and if you aren't wearing a ring, I'm going to come up there and pack your shit into my car and move you out myself."

I wasn't thrilled about moving into the teepee, either, I had to admit, but not because it was a teepee, which can be pretty cozy when properly situated and well outfitted (though that was not the case with this particular teepee). It was big enough, certainly, but instead of the beds being built into its sides in the traditional way, where they could be out of the way of the smoke hole at the top of the structure, Mick's bed—and now my bed—was centered so that is sat directly under the smoke hole, where a wood-stove or fire pit should have been, and because this was northern, coastal California and the teepee sat at the edge of a thick, damp redwood and fir forest, water seeped in from everywhere, especially from the hole in the roof, directly above the bed.

The first night I slept in the teepee, Mick stepped in ahead of me and pulled a heavy blue plastic tarp off the bed, and the sound of at least a gallon of water hitting the ground beneath us—the bare ground—was unmistakable, even in the pitch-black darkness. "Voilà!" he said, with what sounded like a grin. There was something romantic and brave about it then, in my twenty-three-year-old mind, especially at night, when I was lying in the dark under heavy blankets next to him, listening to him talk about what he wanted to build in that clearing and the sort of life he wanted to lead, with horses and children. There was also something very familiar and very comfortable about this bed, this place, this wild collection of plans and dreams, barely separated from the wilderness around it by feeble tarps and blankets, sitting on a damp and cold ground that I knew—but did not want to remind myself—could quietly digest everything, leaving no trace of us at all.

When I moved in with Mick, he had begun to build a small cabin. The teepee was still standing and was now our guesthouse. Nobody was asking to stay over. The cabin would be our home until Mick had built a house for us, which would happen, by his estimation, over the course of the next two or three years. For this reason, the cabin was not in the center of the clearing but at the edge of it, under the trees.

The two-hundred-square-foot cabin had no phone or electricity, but we did have a water tank and a solar-powered pump that supplied a kitchen sink and an outdoor shower. Our outhouse did not have walls, and was hidden from sight—barely—behind trees on the other side of the clearing. We had a small but powerful woodstove for heat and a gas cookstove and lantern, plus a few solar-powered lights by the bed for reading and a solar-powered refrigerator that took up a lot of space but actually didn't work very well. We used it like a big cooler, replacing a big block of ice in the vegetable drawer every few days, which meant carrying a plastic box full of water through the cabin, trying not to spill it as you rushed toward the door. My routine, at least for the first summer and fall at the cabin, was organized around daylight hours: up at dawn, which was when Mick would leave for his shop in town, coffee on my front step, a drive into town for groceries or the occasional drawing or painting class at the College of the Redwoods, the community college I was attending at the time. I walked through the woods in the mornings and learned about the mushrooms that grew there, which included huge amounts of prized chanterelles, which I picked and sent to my cousin in New York City, who used them in the restaurant he managed there—The Red Cat. I cooked a big dinner for us every afternoon, with a small battery-powered radio next to me playing NPR, on a wooden countertop that stood in front of an opening in the wall where a large window would eventually go, gazing out onto my meadow and thinking about the house that would be there.

The woodstove was efficient and the space was small enough that it could be heated pretty quickly, except, of course, for the fact that the cabin was missing this window, which took up most of one wall. Mick had plans to build a craftsman-style window frame by hand, but by the beginning of November it still had not been done, so he hung a sheet of plastic over the window and the doorway (because he also planned to build a door by hand, but that had not happened, either) and the room grew instantly warm, while my view began to disappear.

The outdoor shower's water pressure was so light that when I stood underneath it, I couldn't feel water hitting me but could just feel my head getting heavier and wetter. I got a gym membership (frowned upon by Mick) and began spending a lot of time in town, living in the cabin out of a duffel bag that held my toiletries and the only mirror we owned, which was four inches wide. "I feel like you aren't even living here anymore," he complained, in an increasingly familiar tone of disapproval. Then I—instead of telling him that living on his terms was too hard, especially when he couldn't seem to get a door or a window hung, especially since he went to work every day, at dawn, in a woodshop with a spacious office with a phone and hot coffee, especially since I was really the one living, cooking, being there—begged him for a claw-foot bathtub. He procured one, and we dragged it into the woods and set it up under two big fir trees and found a piece of PVC pipe that was long enough to funnel water from the shower head. We fixed a way to keep it in place long enough to fill the tub, and I spent that winter taking long baths in the evenings and sometimes in the mornings, too, with the rain and sometimes even a bit of snow falling around me, and for a few more months I relaxed into a bare-bones, but beautiful, home.

But as the second winter approached, with still no window or door, I started to panic. I rented a little office in town and had my own phone for the first time in more than a year, and I used it to call my sister regularly. I still spoke with confidence about the cabin; I could be happy there while Mick built a larger house, especially if we had a phone line put in and, of course, I added, if he put the windows and doors in. "The what?" she said, unable to comprehend a house with entire walls missing. I assured her all would be well, but by then I knew that even though Mick went to work at five each morning, he spent most of his day drinking coffee and having long, earnest conversations with his staff and crew, who were also very earnest, and that his company had developed a reputation for being slow to finish the complex jobs they took. "I'm coming up there for Thanksgiving," she said, and hung up.

She didn't ask a lot of questions when she saw the cabin; she didn't need to. I showed her a photo that Mick's sister, a photographer, had taken of it from the side that did have a finished window, with my bathtub in the foreground, which made it all look very beautiful. "I'm not saying it isn't beautiful," my sister said. "It is." I thought I had begun to win her over, but then around Christmastime a letter arrived from her. Inside was a newspaper clipping about the Unabomber, who had sequestered himself in a not-too-far-away wilderness and built himself a cabin, which was pictured in a black-and-white photo, from an angle that showed a single, small window that looked remarkably familiar to me. The clipping contained a note from her, mentioning little else than the fact that the photo had been entered as evidence of the man's utter insanity. The caption read, "Primitive home to the Unabomber, of seven years, just 200 sq. feet!"

My second summer in the cabin was the summer that the bear began coming. When a black bear determines that your house is a good source for food, you've got a real problem. When a black bear determines that your house is a good source for food and your house only has three complete walls, and no front door at all, it's more complicated.

The important thing to know about bears, when you are

defending your home and your food from them, is that they are not acting on instinct when they hunt for their meals. Bears learn everything from their mothers. They are born in the early spring and stay in and near their dens until they are old enough to go foraging. Their mother will then introduce them to every food source that she knows about, and this will happen in the late spring and throughout the summer. A bear will often stay with its mother through another winter and begin to start venturing out on its own the following summer. A mother bear will even teach her cubs to help her steal; they have been known to send cubs up thin trees and out onto weak branches to claw at the ropes that hold hikers' food bags until they fall to the ground. Our bear was a mother bear, with two yearlings, and that was the summer that they found us: two people and a big pile of food sitting on the edge of a clearing.

Mick kept a shotgun under the bed, and always had, though he never used it except on an annual duck-hunting trip with his family and to scare away the errant pest. He had never done much cooking up at the clearing before I moved in, but now the smell of food was everywhere, and the only thing standing in between this four-hundred-pound black bear and her two cubs and our odiferous, not-quite-cold-enough fully stocked fridge, was our bed. That summer was also the summer that we had two small kittens. They had been found, eyes still closed, in the stud cavity of an old barn that Mick had taken down for its lumber. Their mother had moved the rest of the litter but had become too frightened of Mick and his crew and had not come back for these two, so I took them and fed them with tiny bottles and raised them myself. They slept in a box at the foot of my bed, between us and the doorway, with a hot water bottle, which was where they were the first night the bear came.

When I woke up, I could see her shape on our front step with the moonlight behind her, outlining her two round ears. She watched us, probably wondering why we didn't have a front door. She was not more than four feet away from the foot of our bed, and from the kittens, who probably smelled like warm milk to her, a small hot snack. I sat up slowly, and she backed away just a half step. I crawled, holding my breath, on my hands and knees toward her, my long flannel nightgown dragging underneath my knees and slowing me down, until I reached the end of the bed. I reached down and pulled the tiny sleeping kittens out of their box and clutched them to my chest as I jumped back toward my pillow, and screamed as hard as I could, "BEAR!" The bear turned and trotted away, not as quickly as I would have liked. Mick was awake now and mumbling to me. "We need to get a dog," he said.

"We need to get a FUCKING DOOR," I said, still upright in bed, staring into the darkness where the bear had been, clutching the kittens. Mick turned away and went back to sleep.

A day or two later, the kittens (whom I took with me everywhere after the bear began to appear) and I returned to the cabin after dark, following a rare night out (I hated getting home after dark to a cold, dark cabin because seeing it from the outside depressed me). There I found the heavy fridge turned on its side, its contents strewn along the floor of the cabin and on the bed, the plastic bread bags and empty containers and butcher paper spread out in front of the cabin, all licked clean and crushed by big clawed paws, turned from groceries into garbage. A cast-iron pot that had been sitting on the top of the fridge was cracked into two pieces, and broken glass was everywhere. I threatened now to buy a cheap door at the hardware store, but Mick assured me that even if he could allow me to do this, it would not work

To hang your food out of the reach of bears while camping or living with-out a door, first put it into a sleeping bag, stuff sack, or other waterproof sack or bag. Choose a branch from which to hang your food. It should be at least as thick as your upper arm and not dead or dying (look for green leaves or leaf buds on its tips) and it should be at least 10' (3 m) off the ground. Tie one end of a long (at least 30' [10 m]) rope around a rock or other heavy item. Make sure the rock is secure. Stand directly under the branch where you want to hang your food, then take 10 steps backward. Throw the rock over the branch, leaving a loose pile of rope in front of you. This may take a few attempts. When you have succeeded and the rope is over the branch and the rock is safely on the ground again, remove the rock from the rope's end and replace it with your stuff sack, tying it securely with a slipknot. Using the other end of the rope, hoist your stuff sack so that it is about 5' (1.5 m) below your branch, then secure your rope to the tree's trunk, knotting it in a way that can be undone easily.

because the frame that he had built was a custom, not standard, size. Instead, I gathered large, pointy rocks and made a pile of them next to my bed, the way I had been taught to do when camping in bear country, and more or less stopped sleeping at night. Mick began to keep his shotgun, loaded, under his side of the bed. When the bear came back the next time, he pulled it out and charged the bear, firing two shots into the middle of the clearing. I stood in the doorway and watched him, standing naked in the grass, surrounded by the pile of wood that had rotted because there still wasn't a shed, the outhouse that still did not have walls, the warped table that stood next to our fire pit that we had stopped using as a dining table, the lumber that had sat, untouched, exposed, nearly ruined, that was supposed to become our house, and I realized that I couldn't even imagine a building in that clearing anymore, much less a lifetime.

Mick came back to bed. "How much longer do you see us living here, in this cabin?" I asked, in the dark. "Because if we want to have kids"—which he did, very much—"I think we need to start making some changes."

And he, still cold next to me beneath the blankets, having just chased a black bear out of our house, said, "I think we could get by here for another ten years, until the kids are bigger and need more space."

"What about the door?" I asked. "Can you make the door?"

"Yes," he said, "I'll get to it this weekend." But, as I was coming to realize, he always said that.

I found a small house for rent in town and moved us into it, just short of three years since I had arrived. Mick wanted me to promise that we would spend at least a few nights a week at the cabin, but I was done. We lived in mostly silence together for a few months, him constantly criticizing everything about our new, electrified, suburban existence, refusing to partake in general household duties, which seemed mundane and modern to him, insulting his principles. One day, when I arrived unannounced at his shop, I found him engaged in a clearly romantic conversation with a woman he had known for decades. She had professed her longstanding love and admiration for him, and his earnest ways, and within the year she would leave her husband and her home for Mick and his plans to build them a house, in the clearing, on seventy-five acres, where they would live off the land and eventually raise a family together—after a short time in their temporary home, which was a small cabin that lacked a front door, but that, he had assured her, was a simple thing to fix. He would get to it next weekend.

HOW TO
start a children's
clothing company

THE ABSOLUTE BEST TIME TO START a business is when you have nothing to lose. Luckily for me, that was a long and protracted period of my life, from about nine until about thirty-five, when I was neither a mother nor a wife nor shared, in any real way, in the responsibility of maintaining a home or managing the expectations or happiness of anyone but myself. My family expected so little of me from the beginning that I was not burdened with the fear of disappointing them, and they had invested so little in me and in my care and education that they were not in a position to question what I did with my life. I don't think either of my parents knew, when I left college the spring of my senior year, that I had made the decision not to graduate or what my degree would have been in.

My mother had not been in a position to help me financially after I left her house, but every once in a while she made it clear to me that she wanted to. Once, at the beginning of my last year at school, she had brought me a garbage bag of pot, thinking that I could sell it to pay my rent. A friend of hers, a hunter, had been out in the woods on his large property preparing for deer season when he had stumbled across a big, uninvited patch of it and, wanting it off his land, had picked it and brought it to her, thinking that my uncle, a professional of sorts in this field, might be able to sell it. My mother was jealous of her brother for other, older reasons and didn't see why he should benefit from this situation, so she brought it to me, explaining that this was her way of helping. Not wanting to become a drug dealer myself (for obvious reasons, including the fact that the hours seemed ridiculous), I brought it to the one person I knew who openly sold pot in our college town. He told me it was worth next to nothing because it was picked prematurely and offered to take it off my hands, which was by then all I wanted, but I learned later that he had done a brisk business selling it.

My father, on the other hand, had not contributed to my education in any way, even though he had built a successful business in high tech in California. When I moved there from Vermont, he seemed wary of my motives and that I would be asking him for money. He was married for the third time, to a smart but obsessive and high-strung woman who had little patience for his previous wives and their children. I visited him occasionally, usually en route to or from visiting my sister, who had moved back to Santa Cruz, but I never stayed long because his household seemed tense; whether that was because I was there or not, I never knew. My half-brother Cameron was born a year after I arrived in California. I drove south to see him, but when I called my father's house to tell them I was coming, his wife, Michelle, told me that the doctor had told her that nobody but immediate family should come into contact with the baby for at least two weeks. But if I wanted to come over and stand outside, in front of the picture window that faced their driveway, they would hold him up for me to see. I declined.

I was still working at the Environmental Education Center in Mendocino during the spring and fall, having been hired on after my internship, and also as a wilderness guide during the summers and on and off at a horse barn leading rides on the beach and through the foothills of the Mendocino coast. I lived first in a cabin that was included in my job and then in a tiny cottage in Caspar, where I could see the sea from a tiny window by the pillow in my loft bed.

I worked seasonally and had plenty of time for travel and classes, so I enrolled at the local community college, where a renowned textile designer named Lolli Jacobsen happened to be teaching. I took classes in silk-painting and screen-printing from Lolli, plus some printmaking classes from another teacher, and soon had a stack of scarves, T-shirts, and prints on paper, and nothing to do with them. A woman in my screen-printing class had reserved a booth at a local craft fair but didn't have enough money to pay for it, so I shared the cost with her. I arrived an hour before the fair started and spread out a white tablecloth and my shirts and my scarves and my paper prints and everything I had made during my two semesters at College of the Redwoods. The fair started at nine o'clock, and by eleven I had nothing left. I had in my hands a stack of cash, just over a thousand dollars. I was twenty-three years old and could count on one hand the number of times that I'd had this much money to my name. It occurred to me that I should stay in art school forever, but I already had student loans that I could barely manage. Instead, I went to Mexico, back to San Miguel, for the winter, the one place I knew I could live as an artist on $1,100, where a winter's worth of art classes would cost me just $150.

I studied textiles, which was what interested me the most, and learned about dyes and printing, looms and weaving.

I learned, finally, about the relationships between colors. I supported myself in Mexico as an artist's model at the National Art School, which meant spending long hours standing, reclining, and sitting naked in a cold room in an old stone hacienda for artists from every country including mine. Our teacher was Antonio Lopez Vega, perhaps one of the best-known living artists working in Mexico at that time. I could never tell, because my Spanish was so bad, if he liked me too much or not at all, and when I left the city he owed me more money than he wanted to give me, so he paid me in part with two paintings, both of me. "Someday," he told me, "when you have children who have children, you will look at these and you will remember when you were young and poor and took your clothes off for food." I think he meant this differently than it sounded—I was not doing *that* kind of work—but I accepted them and rolled them up into a tube and sent them home to my sister. Upon opening them, she drove straight to the bank without even taking a minute to put on her shoes and deposited money into my account. I returned to California in the spring certain that it was possible to make a living as an artist but not having any idea how.

I was still on the periphery of my father's life, not at all a part of its daily routine, and not at all liked or accepted by his wife, but he had started to take a genuine interest in what I was up to and offered to help me in some small but significant ways. He sent me two hundred dollars while I was in Mexico to help pay for the silver that I needed for a jewelry class, and then helped me buy a car when the one I had purchased for eight hundred dollars finally died, asking me not to tell his wife that he had given me any money. He was worried, as my sister was, when I left Mendocino and moved in with Mick in Arcata and started talking about "living off the land." He called me from his crackly cell phone one morning, just after I told him what I was planning to do. "The thing about that lifestyle, Heather, is that it's very unfair to the women who enter into it. You won't be making any money of your own, and you'll be working hard just to feed yourself and to stay alive, and it's hard, physical work. You are talented and smart, and you should be doing something creative. I think you could get work designing websites. I'm sending you a computer and a tablet and I want you to learn how to use Photoshop." It didn't occur to either of us at the time that I wouldn't have any place to plug the devices in.

The computer was the reason, the final justification that I needed while living with Mick, to rent a desk in a small office in town and set myself up with a telephone. The Internet was literally brand new, and e-mail was only just becoming a normal way to communicate, much less to do business. My father found me a potential freelance job that required Photoshop, so I stayed up all night and burned through two headlamp batteries reading *Photoshop for Dummies* and spent the next day trying to do the work expected of me, but I didn't have any training in graphic design or page layout and wasn't able to produce anything that looked right or appealed to the client.

When things with Mick fell apart, I realized that I needed to find a way to support myself. I had believed, when I moved in with him, that I had discovered a shortcut by teaming up with a man who was happy to support me, who already owned land and had an established career, and that this meant I wouldn't need to find my own career path. But by the time we had broken up, I knew that I never wanted to depend on someone like that again.

It was around then that I stumbled upon a catalog from the Dutch company Oilily. The images were beautiful, full of red-cheeked children with tousled hair, wearing clothing in beautifully printed fabrics with rich embroidery and other tiny, exquisite details. I must have looked at every page close to a hundred times, and I reached the decision that I would start a children's clothing company. I knew I needed help and asked my sister and my father to get involved. We visited a consultant in San Francisco who gave us a basic description of how the apparel industry worked: We needed a brand, and a line, and then we needed to bring that line to a trade show and get orders from retailers, which we would then need to fill. At the time there were still manufacturers in California who were willing to sew what we knew would be small amounts of clothing for us, but there were signs that the situation was changing. We ignored those signs.

Then I began to design my own prints. I went to a local art store and picked out eight colors from their assortment of high-quality art markers. There was a buttery yellow, a warm orange, a grass green, a hot, hot pink, a deep reddish brown, a sky blue, a peachy pink, and a pale, pale aqua. Using only these colors and a stack of thick drawing paper, I designed five prints. One of them was a simple design of small white clouds in a white sky, based on a batik T-shirt that my mother had owned, a gift from my aunt in Brooklyn. Another was a simple design of pink tulips, taken from the coveted Laura Ashley wallpaper design that hung in the bedroom of Jill Higgins, the richest girl I had ever known. A third was of geese, straight from the Jemima Puddle-Duck illustration on the page in Kerry Canfield's Beatrix Potter address book that held my long list of crossed-out addresses. Another was of tiny little girls, inspired by a vintage print that I had found in an old quilt. My favorite was a print of tiny little apples, in green, just like the ones that had grown on the tree in front of the schoolhouse. Then, using a San Francisco phone book, I called every screen printer in the Bay Area until I found one who was willing to make a set of screens for me and another who would print my fabric. The latter was a woman in San Francisco who had a very keen sense of color, which was much more important than I could have imagined at that moment.

I had promised the man who was going to make the screens that I would provide him with Photoshop files, so I used the old Wacom tablet and Mac that my father had given me to redraw my print designs and send the files via e-mail. It would be weeks before I would have sample fabric, so I started working on some very basic dresses, using plain cotton and muslin. I made a simple tie-top dress, based entirely on the one that my mother had brought me back from France, tucked into a box of cigarettes; a pair of pants; a dress; a blouse inspired by the perfectly proportioned pieces in the Oilily catalog; and a few other simple little things. When my fabric came back, I had a friend who had worked in fashion in Los Angeles help me make the patterns, and then another friend, a seasoned seamstress, make some samples. I had my very first collection. I knew that I wanted to introduce my line in New York, at the biggest kid's clothing trade show, but a booth would cost me just over four thousand dollars. My father had given me another car, a hand-me-down Ford Explorer, which was still worth about ten thousand dollars. I took the title to a local economic development corporation and borrowed money against it, and I bought a booth space and round-trip airline tickets and booked a hotel. I hired a photographer to take some pictures of little girls wearing my clothes, including a little girl in a sundress made from my apple print, sitting on a giant red beanbag, with tousled blond hair and rosy cheeks. I had blowups of these made, three feet square and mounted on foam core, and I punched holes in the corners so that I could hang them on the walls of my simple booth. I made up a name—Munki Munki—over lunch at a Chinese restaurant, where I had been accidentally given two paper placemats with the Chinese astrological signs on them. Where they overlapped, I could see two monkeys next to each other and thought the name sounded sweet in repeat. I changed the spelling to something that sounded remotely Dutch, in honor of Oilily.

I shipped the blowups to New York with some simplified catalogs called line sheets—I had just found out what these were and that I would be needing them, and had had them printed at Kinkos—and followed, with my samples in my suitcase, behind them. I hired someone to help me, a smart girl named Melissa, who was supportive and sweet. A few days before we left for New York, she looked at me and said, "You have lost so much weight that you look like a different person." I had gotten quite fat living with Mick, finding some happiness in food, but now I wasn't cooking for him or for myself and hadn't eaten a solid meal in weeks.

Melissa also showed me how to use spell check. The first time I turned it on, I saw the e-mail I was working on (to a potential sales rep) light up like a Christmas tree, its errors underlined in red and green lines and highlights. I had never had a job that required spelling skills. We laughed at the words that I had spelled wrong, including "apparel" and "palette."

My booth was no-frills except for its coveted corner location. Setting it up was simple: I hung my blowups and draped my fabrics over tables and then walked back to my hotel, not knowing what the coming days would bring. I had my hair cut that night for the first time in five years. I had it colored, too, and then I went into a discount department store and bought a dress and a cardigan sweater that seemed to say "trade show." I hadn't ever had a job that was indoors, except for waitressing and the job that hadn't required any clothing at all, so even though I was a clothing designer now, I was myself a mismatched mess.

The first day of the show was a blur. We had never been to a trade show before, so we didn't know whether we were busy or not, and we didn't know, at least at first, if our experience was unique. Someone sat down to write an order, then someone else, then suddenly, all eight chairs were filled, and then there were more customers standing in line. It wasn't until I ran to the bathroom that I saw that nobody else had a line. There was finally a break near the end of the day, so I took a calculator and added up the numbers. I had to do it twice before I believed it. I had, on my lap, almost fifty thousand dollars in orders.

That first show yielded more than eighty thousand dollars in orders, plus many promising leads. I went home in a state of joy and shock, and began building a production process and a business around that stack of orders. I went back to my lender and borrowed more, scrambling for collateral, using my sister's car title and a chunk of money from a friend as guarantees. The business was growing quickly; everyone loved the designs (until they didn't), and everyone wanted to be a part of what was happening.

First came the partners. Then came the factories, then the bigger space and the new computers and the warehouse shelves and the lawyers. Then came the arguments, the damaged merchandise, the fall collection that wasn't very good, and the late deliveries. Then our little bank was bought by an even bigger bank, which saw us as a liability. And then the factories in Los Angeles began to shut down. And then came the dot-com bust that brought the whole state to its knees. Then the partners were gone, and it was just me again, and not much else. And suddenly it had been seven years. And then, when I knew it was all coming to a close, but didn't yet know how it would end, I found those eight markers. They were all dried out at the tips and their caps were faded, but I could still see their colors on the bands at their bases. In that mess of inventory and heartache and anger and debt, they reminded me, just for a moment, how small and earnest my beginning had been.

I had always believed that if I could be successful, my family would accept and include me, and be proud of me. Until I failed. It was surprising to me that the thing that changed the way my family, especially my father, felt about me wasn't the level of success that I had—briefly—achieved, but rather the courage that I had displayed in trying something that was, it turned out, almost impossible. The failure that followed didn't erase the pride or respect that I had earned; if anything, it galvanized the relationships that I had built with my father and my sister. This is the thing about failure that surprised me, that still surprises me. It is a silent, invisible thing. Failure is running out of gas on a dark dirt road and walking home in the moonlight, the walk itself not ever as bad as the worrying about it was, the watching of the little red needle as it plunged below the empty line for those last few unbearably long miles; instead, the walk is oddly peaceful, and as you wonder why you have suddenly begun to feel so calm, you realize that the fear isn't there anymore.

And, as any successful person will tell you, it is not failure that brings you enemies and adversaries but success. Failure makes you humble. It builds you up in ways that success cannot; it shows you your strengths and teaches you and those around you what you are, who you are. And even if I didn't know it then, I had become an artist, a designer, and an "entreprenuer."

Damn, I still don't know how to spell that word.

HOW TO
make sugar on snow

MAPLE SUGARING SEASON, IN case you did not grow up in the Northeast, is only a few weeks long. It occurs in that brief window of time each spring when the days are beginning to warm but the nighttime temperatures are still below freezing, before the tiny green buds begin to appear on the bare branches of trees. In the lower part of New England, this happens in February, but in northern Vermont, it can start as late as March. Sugar maples realize that it's going to be spring soon and start producing a watery sap that they send up to their branches. If you drive a hollow metal spout into the tree, it will intercept some of this sap, enough to fill a big tin bucket in just a day when things really get going, without harming the tree. And if you boil down the sap in that big bucket on the woodstove, you will get a cup or so of thick maple syrup.

Sugarhouses, where sap is collected and boiled into syrup in big vats, are often out in the woods among the maples that produce the sap, and when you see the thin lines of woodsmoke coming off the hills and from the edges of pastures, their sources barely visible through the still-bare trees, you know that it is the end of winter. It's necessary to enlist help in sugaring, especially when you are boiling down vast quantities of sap in an evaporator fueled with wood that must first be cut and chopped, and when you must stay up all night to keep your fire burning to boil these huge vats of sap and then syrup. Sugarhouses have no insulation and big openings in their roofs, protected by peaked little cupolas, through which the smoke can escape, but during this week of sugaring, their insides are warm and full of sweet-smelling steam and laughing men, happy to be out of their houses.

A few years after I moved to Arcata, I visited my mother and my uncle Mike just before the sugaring season began. There was still thick snow on the ground on the mountain, but the days were clear and sunny, and the air no longer felt frozen and lifeless, even though there were still no buds on the trees or mud on the ground. In town, below, the snow had even begun to melt off driveways and walkways, but on the mountain, it had not given up even a square inch. Mike was trying to get his sugaring operation going again after a few years of dormancy. I drove my completely un-snow-worthy rental car up the steep and snowy dirt road to his farm and found him on the road in front of the sugarhouse, towing an enormous and brand-new evaporator behind a borrowed ATV. When I pulled the car over and opened the door, he cut the engine, jumped off, and ran toward me. I put my arms around him. Even though he felt cold, thin, and tired—not at all what his joyful mood conveyed—I recognized in him the sure signs, the hope and the enthusiasm, that he was, at least for now, clean.

Mike's farm had once been a thriving, wondrous thing, with

a beautiful, massive house and many worked acres, all on top of a mountain. My mother and Mike had both been brought to this area, specifically to The Red House, as teenagers on summer breaks from their boarding schools. Later, they had both run back here, away from their respective colleges, inspired by the back-to-the-land movement, to ask my grandfather for pieces of the mountain, which they were eventually given. Mike was just eighteen when he claimed the Combses' original homesite and, with only books to guide him, built that beautiful timber and stone house with his own hands. His home became a haven for other young, idealistic dropouts, many of them friends from one of the many boarding schools that he had been shuffled among and expelled from, or from Virginia, where his parents were officially living at that time. It was always full of guests, drinking wine and talking—"dreaming out loud," as one of them would say—about a revolutionary way of thinking, of living, of being. One of these young men was my father, who first had been drawn to Mike and his ambitious plans to build a house and a self-sustained way of life in northern Vermont and then had met my mother. She used to say, behind their backs, that my father had fallen in love with Mike first. They looked alike, my mother and Mike, tall and lean and strong, with thick, dark-red hair and green eyes, and honey-colored skin that tanned in the summertime in a freckled pattern that looked like the slick, dappled coat of a wild animal. They were both beautiful and had many admirers, and they both had quick, violent tempers.

I was so young when my parents divorced that the wedding pictures had been stuffed into the woodstove long before I ever thought to ask to see them. I didn't even know how they had ended up married until I was in college, when my mother and I were making dinner and a friend of mine, Mary, came by with a bag of artisan lettuces that she had picked from her garden. "I brought mesclun," she said, holding up the bag of greens.

"Oh, for Christ's sake," my mother said, "I haven't done mescaline since the day I got engaged to Heather's father." My mother spoke openly and bitterly of the deal her parents had offered her, that if she got married she would be given a piece of the mountain, which is how she and my father came to have the dome site. My grandfather took it back when they abandoned it. My father told me once that his decision to marry my mother was due in part to the draft policies of the Vietnam War, but in the end he was drafted anyway, when my sister and I were just four days old. He managed to avoid being sent overseas by intentionally failing his medical exam, but his trick was eventually discovered. He then went to Canada, where he and other draft dodgers lived for a while in Sutton, a small town just a few miles past the border crossing, where they helped to run a Montessori school attended by their own children, brought over daily by the wives and girlfriends left in Vermont. I remember these caravans faintly—me and a pile of other small children in the backs of cars—and I remember that sometimes my father was there when we got to the school, and sometimes he was not. This was the beginning of my father's series of long absences, and then of his legal problems (stemming from a minor drug-possession arrest), the end of the dome, the end of his marriage to my mother, and, eventually, the end of his time as a member of my mother's family and on the mountain. He left for good on a very cold, gray day. My mother, with my sister and me in the car, drove him to the nearest highway and left him, with his backpack, on the edge of the road to hitch his way to California, where he thought he might be able to find work and then, he promised, help support us. We waved to him, my sister and I, from behind the small, oval rear window of our rusty little Saab, and he waved back, standing next to a guardrail, with no other car in sight. My father and I would reconnect again when we were both older and able to understand one another as adults. He had been just nineteen when he married my mother, and barely twenty when my sister and I were born. At that age, he could imagine that almost anything was possible, but then, I had to assume, he decided that none of it was.

By the time my father left the mountain, The Red House had begun its tenure as summerhouse to my aunts and uncles and their children, changing the culture of the mountain at least seasonally and eliminating Mike's precious privacy for part of the year. In the summer, we would run down to his house in a small, barefoot pack and burst through the door without even knocking, and play in his barn and his pastures. In the wintertime, when my cousins were gone, my sister and I would visit him with our mother, and we would fall asleep with the big pile of dogs that lined up like logs in front of his massive stone fireplace while the adults stayed up late and drank beer and smoked cigarettes. They still talked of revolutionary ideas and lives, but now there was also something else, something less hopeful, picked from a list of things that seemed to be working against them. In the early spring, when Mike sugared, we would spend long hours playing in the snow while my mother helped him collect and boil sap, and he would tell us to bring him a snowball, and he would pour hot syrup onto it, which would freeze and become sticky, and we would eat it all, holding it with both hands, until we were chewing on our own mittens.

When we were twelve or thirteen, he married Mary, the woman who built the riding ring between the barn and the house and gave us all lessons. Her marriage to Mike was one of extremes. Together they had gardens and horses and beauty—in the evenings, after our long rides, I would sit on the porch with them and look out over that green valley, our situation higher even than the mountains on its other side, and I would think to myself, *This is the life that I want, someday.* But then, in the middle of the night, Mary would come to our house and sit with my mother, her head in her hands, and sometimes she would be covered with cuts and bruises.

Drugs had always been at the center of activity at Mike's house. He grew huge amounts of pot on that land, one of his main sources of income for many years. Other sorts of drugs found their way to his home, too, bought and sold and shared among an increasingly rough crowd of dealers that thrived along the Canadian border. Mike's drug use had always been an issue, but during these years it evolved steadily into a full-blown addiction, his lifetime divided by its cycles. When he was high, he was vacant and numb, a benign ghost in his own house and to his wife and the animals who depended on him, avoiding us unless he needed something. When the money and the drugs were all used up, he would fall into a bitter, desperate place and become cruel to everyone around him, or there would be an event—an illness, an overdose, an accident, his divorce—that would finally force him to come clean, to get enough rest and enough clarity and humility to rebuild for a time, to impress us with his strength, his beauty, his mind. And then there would be a period of hope, and there would be a new woman—always, a woman—in his house. These women loved him wholly, almost fatally. To them, he was more myth than man. The potential and the promise that he seemed to offer, of this extraordinary life with an extraordinary man, seemed to blind them. They worked tirelessly, each of them, to build lives with him in that remote place, to survive there with him, and then, too many times, to survive *him*. Always, they left broken and tired. But none of them, I believe, would ever stop loving him, would ever fully regain her sight. One of these women, Stacey, was the older sister of a high school friend. I remember visiting Mike during sugaring season my first year of college. He was just past forty then, but still handsome, still strong, even though we suspected that he was ill. He was alone in the sugarhouse when I found him, boiling sap for the third day without rest. I asked him to make me a sugar-on-snow, more out of habit than out of wanting one, but he ignored me.

"Stacey is pregnant," he said. He seemed genuinely happy and went on to tell me that she was moving in with him, that this had been put off for too long, and that now he was ready. I knew that he was also telling me that he was going to be clean, that he wasn't going to be a junkie anymore. "I'm going to have Butternut bred, get the horse thing going again. I like the idea of having a colt or a filly coming next spring, and growing up alongside of this baby, you know, Tupy? Fresh start." But Stacey left him just a few weeks later, and while I never knew the reasons she had for leaving, it was easy enough for me to imagine why she went before having her baby, whom she named Will. I met him once, when he was very small. Stacey put him in my arms, this little cousin. She was sober now and in love with someone else, and they were happy, and safe.

A few years later, on a bitterly cold day in February, Mike's house was badly damaged by a fire, caused by an electrical failure in a set of grow lights, under which he insisted he had been starting tomatoes. He and his newest girlfriend, Jeannie, whom I found impossible to like or trust, had hauled a school bus up the mountain road, parked it next to the house, now blackened and under tarps, and moved into it, heating it with a woodstove, while they began trying to rebuild. I visited them there on a rainy day in the summer. They were growing and storing impressive amounts of food and keeping cows, goats, pigs, and sheep, and as long and as beautiful as summer days on this mountaintop still were, they could do nothing but dedicate almost every minute to preparing for the next nine or ten months, a frantic attempt at surviving another winter on a mountaintop in a narrow steel bus. A place that had once felt like a hidden paradise, high above the rest of the world, now seemed to me inhospitable, barely survivable, and dangerous.

My grandmother died a few years later, and when I went to Mike's to take him to her funeral—he had no working car now, no license, no insurance, and he and Jeannie were barely surviving on the mountain—we argued because they insisted on smoking in my car even though I had asked them not to. I wouldn't have minded, but it was borrowed from friends who were sure to notice. "Goddamn it, Tupy," he said, angry from the backseat. "This is Vermont. Everybody smokes here." The only thing keeping him from using drugs to endure what seemed to be a miserable, inescapable event, I gathered, was that he was broke.

But when I saw him again, on that spring day years later when he was towing the evaporator, he seemed to have forgotten that memory and that he had been angry with me. He had been left a little bit of money by my grandfather who had died the previous fall, and he was using it to try to get his farm operational again. He was full of fresh hope, even though he was sick with the hepatitis C that he had already lived with for a decade, and he was thin and gaunt, almost all of the handsome gone, some of the teeth missing from his smile. He talked with his eyes wide and his hands held open toward me, in constant motion. They were rough and dirty, like his clothes, and he smelled of stale cigarettes, but he was *clean*. Jeannie came up behind him and said hello with a brusque, awkward hug, and immediately made a comment about my coat, which was warmer than hers, and then said something obnoxious about my car, which was a fancy rental ill-suited to these roads. I was actually a little surprised that I had made it up the road without snow tires, which I had insisted on when making the reservation but hadn't been given at the airport. "Yes," I said, "I told the lady at Hertz that I would probably total it." Even after agreeing with her about both points, I remained, in her eyes, just one of the summer people, the relatives of Mike's who came in their nice cars to stay at The Red House. It bothered me that, now that I had gone and come back, I was so easily dismissed as an outsider in this place. In *this* place. I offered to cook them both dinner at my mother's house later that night.

I made a hearty soup and soft bread for dinner. Jeannie and Mike arrived after dark, in a new truck, after they had lost the daylight needed to work at the sugarhouse, which still didn't have power but would soon. We sat around the small, round table. Mike talked about his plans for the coming spring and summer: His house would be rebuilt, his gardens would be producing fresh and canned goods, he would have horses again, I could come riding the next time I came. He was clean, he said, nothing but canned beer and cigarettes, and no junk, not anymore. And then Mike asked me if he had ever told me about the first time he had been high. It was when he was in boarding school, in Switzerland, where his parents had placed him at the age of five, just as World War II ended. The first time they left him there, they did not come back until Christmas. In later years, they stopped coming to visit him entirely. It was during one of these holidays, when he was left with limited supervision in an almost empty dormitory, the youngest not to have been called home for Christmas, that the older boys had refused to share their drinks with him, pushing him out into an empty hallway and telling him that he could go into the kitchen and find some nutmeg to smoke. "That was it," he said, leaning back in his chair, a cigarette in one hand. "That was it." I left the next morning at dawn, in a snowstorm, but I missed my flight because I crashed the rental car into a guardrail near Belvedere Bog. I had to sit in the Burlington airport for six hours, surrounded by literature about Vermont businesses and ads for maple syrup. That was when I began dreaming about a way to help Mike sell his syrup.

It was easy enough to get a meeting with the bulk foods buyer at the Arcata Co-op. My story was a good one: I was representing a small farmer who used traditional (if not primitive) methods. He was interested and gave me much more time and attention than I deserved, but he already had a supplier: Shady Maple Farms. This is where I crossed the line. "Shady Maple?" I said, eyebrows up and voice lowered to convey my corporate horror. "You do know about them, right?"

"No, *what* about them?" he asked. I had nothing. I was just hoping to hit a socially conscious nerve, hoping that there *was* something wrong with Shady Maple, some fact that he already felt guilty about but was knowingly ignoring. He stared back at me, waiting for the bad news about his trusted, longstanding supplier. "Let's just say they put the *shady* in *maple*," I said, nodding slowly and squinting a little. That did it. I had an order for fourteen massive plastic casks of my uncle's maple syrup, which was what Mike said he could deliver. That was worth more than four thousand dollars. The fact that they would be buying and selling it in bulk was important; Mike wasn't equipped to sterilize, fill, seal, and ship small bottles of syrup safely or profitably, so he needed a buyer who would take all of his syrup in these casks instead of fancy little bottles with labels.

It took me almost an hour to convince UPS to send a driver up the long dirt road to my uncle's place to pick up all of that syrup, through all of that snow, carrying a check from me in the amount of four thousand dollars. Meanwhile, the co-op wanted a logo and company description for the store's big wooden bulk container. I called Mike with the news and offered to make one. "OK, you can make a logo, but don't give me that cutesy moose and cow crap," Mike had said. "I want something real, something that shows what Vermont is *really* like." We agreed that Mike's was not a lifestyle that could or should be depicted on a bulk foods bin, so I went for humor instead and drew a little man carrying a tin bucket, humming as he walked through his woods, unaware of the massive, salivating black bear behind him. He loved it. He told me that when he first saw it, he laughed and laughed and laughed. My mother loved it, too. I consider this—making two rather cynical Vermonters laugh in what must have been March—to be a great personal artistic achievement. I told everyone in town, everyone that I knew, that the maple syrup in the bulk department at the co-op was from my *family*. My *mountain*. I didn't let myself think about the fact that I had given Mike four thousand dollars, that he had just worked with very little sleep, for weeks, in the snow, splitting wood for and then tending the fires that needed to burn day and night to boil down all of that syrup, backbreaking work in freezing weather that would be followed by a period of nothing but waiting for spring, which, when you are an addict with four thousand dollars in your pocket, is likely more temptation, more justification, than you need to slip back onto familiar ground, to disappear, to rest, to let go of what you have, just for a moment.

When I talked to my mother the following Christmas, she told me that she and Mike had argued about something, that he and Jeannie were "up to their old tricks," that they were desperate again. I ignored these clues and asked her if they were sugaring, but she couldn't tell me. "Can you ask them?" I said. "Please?" Mike didn't have a phone, so I was asking her to drive up to their place, which I knew she didn't want to do. Mike called me a few days later from a pay phone. "Listen, Heather, I can get you syrup again, right?" his voice was gritty, strained, and tired. "But look, you know, you have to pay me something upfront, so I can get it made, and hey, if I was L.L.Bean, and you wanted some boots, well, you would have to send me the money first and then I'd send you the boots, right?" He had obviously been searching in his own blurry mind for a way to rationalize what he was doing, knowing that it was my money that I was sending, that the Arcata Co-op paid a month or so after it was shipped the syrup, and that it wasn't enough to have the check arrive on the same day that the syrup was collected, that he needed it now, months in advance. I said I'd do it, and even though I set up a wire transfer, even though it took no more than two days for the cash to reach him, it didn't come fast enough, and he called me again and again, sounding more and more desperate each time, from the bank parking lot, from the gas station, wanting to know where it was.

My mother called me a few weeks later, angry. She had lent him money, she said, at Christmastime, so that he could hire help to cut firewood and get set up to sugar, but now, when he was supposed to be making syrup, he wasn't. I told her that she was wrong, that the season hadn't started yet, and she told me that I didn't know what the hell I was talking about, that I was "fucking blind." I hung up on her.

Mike's syrup arrived, as promised, but it came in different casks, was packaged differently than before, and tasted different. There was less of it than there was supposed to be. Later, we learned that Mike had used the money my mother had given him to buy syrup from an old friend, a neighbor who had given him his lower-grade syrup at wholesale, which is what ended up in the bulk bins at the Arcata Co-op that year under the laminated sign that I had made. My money, I had to admit to myself now, had likely gone straight into his arm.

The following Christmas came and went, with no word from Mike. The next winter, my mother told me that he was sugaring again, with the help of a new neighbor who had just built a house on the road to his house, and whom she didn't trust at all. I was too distracted by my own situation—my business was suffering and my relationship with John, my boyfriend, had hit the first of many rocky patches—to see if he wanted to try selling his syrup again. My mother was still angry about the money he hadn't paid back.

John and I had decided to take a trip together, to a remote and rustic hotel in the Caribbean, which was how it came to be that when I got the call that Mike had died, I was sitting in bright, blinding sunshine. This made it all the more difficult, almost impossible, to imagine a man, thin and sick, dying alone in his hard-won sleep on the top of a snowy, dark mountain, in the middle of sugaring season, after days of getting no rest and working hard in the bitterly cold winter air.

It hurt too much to imagine, at that moment, in the sun,

the way the bus must have looked that night, with the ruined stone house next to it, or the once-new truck, no longer running, parked nearby, all of it under several feet of snow. Or the long walk that Jeannie made after she found him, in the middle of the night, past the road that had led to the now-empty Red House, the abandoned and overgrown dome site, and Donald's little tin shack. She'd walked a mile and a half in the dark, all the way through the woods to the neighbor's house, all without the dogs, who wouldn't leave Mike's side.

I can see it all now, clearly, in my mind. Enough years have gone by, and I've managed to accept it as the final chapter in a story about a place where we had all dreamt out loud.

HOW TO
save a drowning child (part II)

MAURA WAS MY THERAPIST. Technically, she billed herself as an entrepreneurial advisor, which made it easier to tell John, my boyfriend of three years, that I was seeing her, since he and his family believed mental or emotional weaknesses to be the worst, most unerasable, irrevocable sort of stigma. He was young—six years my junior—and only partly American, his mother being from Sweden, and he came from a family that was good in every way except this one. While I could forgive them for it because I knew that the United States was unique in its obsessive embrace of mental maladies, and because I loved them, it was inconvenient because I really, really needed help.

Maura had been recommended to me by my good friend Wendy, who, like me, managed her own precarious business, a very popular, very good restaurant. We had been friends for almost as long as I had lived in Arcata. Not only had I made her wedding dress, but I had also bought it back from her for four dollars at her post-divorce yard sale a few years later. "Don't take it too personally," a mutual friend of ours said to me, holding up a pack of tarot cards, as we both stood in line to pay for our armloads of souvenirs from Wendy's soon-to-be-former life. "I gave her these for her birthday last year."

Wendy's childhood had been about as unsteady as my own. "One time," she told me over a bottle of wine, "we moved into a new house," she took a sip of wine, "in the snow," another sip, "without a car." We could compare stories like these and, when our lives were going well, be proud of ourselves. When things were not going well, especially in our businesses, we told them to each other for a different reason: to commiserate, in some way, about how very lonely and vulnerable we felt and how frightening it was to be so utterly dependent on ourselves and no one else. We had both learned to take care of ourselves from terrible teachers, and we were attracted to crisis because it was familiar to us. When Wendy told me that Maura had helped her and that I could be helped, too, I believed her. I knew that Maura had assisted Wendy in righting and then selling her business and getting out of a marriage that seemed, from the outside, to be good but really was not.

I liked to pretend that the sofa in Maura's office was one of the chaise lounges I had seen in psychiatrist's offices in movies, even though it was a short, fluffy two-seater with big rolled arms from IKEA. I would lie on it with my legs hanging off the end closest to her face, my head flat on the seat cushion, staring up at her ceiling. I had learned by then that I was especially prone to visual distractions, that when it came to my brain's ability to prioritize its competing stimuli, whatever I was looking at cut to the front of the frontal-lobe queue, and that staring at a blank white wall or ceiling was the only way I could think through complex problems. Maura would sometimes lean forward and put her forehead into my peripheral vision when she was making a point or confronting me about the problems that I seemed to be unable to make go away, which in her opinion were usually the ones (a) that required me to make big and difficult changes and (b) that I would probably repeat for the rest of my life. My main problems, it had become clear to both Maura and me after three or four months together, were that my relationship and my business, both of which had showed so much promise early on, were failing and were probably beyond saving. I was so deeply entrenched in both, so heavily invested in them, that without them I would be starting over with less than nothing. I would have no home—John and I lived together in a house that was in his name—and I would have no job, in a town with very few jobs for a … what was I? I couldn't even imagine what I would do next. And then there were the cats. Just thinking about leaving them behind was enough to make me stay, even though I knew that staying for the cats was legitimately crazy.

My business was just barely staying afloat. We were successful in terms of our product—our collection of children's clothing made from fabrics printed with my own designs was well received and sought after and even collected—but we were failing on nearly every other front. My partners had left, my debts were huge, and the printing houses, cut-and-sew factories, and wash houses that my manufacturing processes depended on were shutting down, one by one, in a final wave of blows to California's apparel industry delivered via Enron and fallout from the bursting tech bubble. I had crossed almost every line I could think of. I'd sold my car to pay for a trade show, I'd dumped cartons of merchandise on discounters, I'd started trying to manufacture things in-house, marketing them as handmade. It had become my full-time job just to bring in enough cash to cover my monthly overhead. There was no time for design or development or thinking beyond the next pay period. Yet, somehow, this reality was an easier one to face, day by day, than accepting that I had actually failed. So I kept going. What frightened me most was this cycle that seemed to be repeating itself, beginning with nothing, building a life with someone, in a new place, and then feeling it begin to fail, watching it come apart. What, I would ask Maura, am I doing wrong?

John had never been in a real relationship before, which meant that he didn't have enough experience to recognize two very important things about me: one, that being embarrassed by the things that your partner says and does in social settings is pretty standard, and two, that what we had between us was, on the scale of great love, pretty spectacular. I never doubted that he loved me because it was the sort of love that I could feel from across the room. I also knew, unfortunately, that he didn't like me at all. I was not organized or neat enough, I didn't take care of my things well enough, I paid too much for cheese, and I often smelled bad, by his standards. I was also too loud, talked too much, especially about myself and my business, and asked too many personal questions. And my work, oh how he hated my work. He didn't want to hear about how difficult my job was or how much stress I was under. Clearly, I had put myself in this position and my priorities were all wrong anyway, so why did I care so much? And why couldn't I just work for someone else—did I think I was so special? And why did my job involve so much self-promotion? That was clearly a sign, he told me again and again, that I was insecure. Once, when we had made a terrible mistake and delivered flawed merchandise to a major catalog customer and they threatened to sue us for the lost income and the cost of printing the product in their catalog,

I broke down on John, hoping that he would show me just the tiniest bit of empathy.

"I might be bankrupt," I tried, and then, instantly afraid that this would make him want to leave me, reassured him by saying, "I guess it's a good thing we aren't married."

"I wouldn't be that stupid," he said, and walked out of the room.

I understood that he was tired of it; I was tired of it, too. But it wasn't just the lows that he wasn't interested in sharing; he didn't seem to care about the highs, either. In fact, they were just as embarrassing to him. One of the few things that I had become very good at was drawing with a computer stylus. This skill translated beautifully in exactly one instance outside of my job: Pictionary. I could draw, of course, but more importantly, I could draw without looking at exactly what I was drawing. John and I played Pictionary together one night with our close friends Tim and Lisa. Tim's older brother, TC, was visiting, so we were two uneven teams. I drew, with my eyes averted, a near-perfect frying pan. Tim and Lisa applauded even though they weren't on my team. TC was especially impressed. John scowled at me the whole way home. "I don't know why you always have to show off," he said, and then, as if on cue, still staring ahead at the road, "My mom thinks it's because you are insecure."

Once, while searching for an idea for a product that would involve my artwork silkscreened onto ready-made goods and after eating an entire bag of stale Halloween candy for lunch, I decided that I should design scratch-and-sniff underwear that depicted men whom I had known and loved and featured, at least through twenty to thirty washes, their signature scents. Carpenter? Cedar. Surfer? Suntan lotion, but only because they didn't make bong. Carnie? Cotton candy. The novelty of the product caught on, and a sample somehow found its way onto the desk of Brendan Koerner, who was writing the column called "The Goods" for the *New York Times* Sunday edition. Two months and an awkward interview later, I woke on a Sunday morning to find myself and my underpants on the cover of the Business section of the *New York Times*. The *New York Times*. For a product that I had designed while high on Kit Kats and desperation, but still. The *New York Times*. I went to the market and bought all ten copies of the newspaper, but when I got home, I took only one of them inside. John and I were meeting his parents, avid *Times* readers, for brunch, and while I was determined not to bring attention to myself, which I knew now that they thought to be a sign of insecurity, I was certain that they would find it themselves and find it at least to be funny, if not a little bit impressive. I had showed it to John already and gotten a lukewarm congrats, and now the paper sat on the table in front of all of us. His father had picked through it already but had not seen the article. How could he have missed it? Coffee came, then eggs, then more coffee, then tea, then the check. Finally, I pulled the section out of the pile, carefully folded it into thirds, and put it into my bag. I told myself that it was the fact that it was about other men, and of course, underpants, indeed scratch-and-sniff underpants, that kept John from showing his parents, or that maybe he had just forgotten. Or perhaps he worried that this was just another opportunity to embarrass myself, which maybe it was. "But come on," I later complained to Wendy and Lisa, "it was the fucking *New York Times*."

On Monday morning I got into my car and there they were, still sitting untouched on the passenger seat. I took my stack of newspapers to work with me, where about three hundred orders for scratch-and-sniff underpants from *New York Times* readers were waiting for me. My friend and screen printer, Tad, tried making the orders for me, but after a week he appeared in my office, where we had already moved on to new, more pressing crises, his arms full of scent-less underpants. "We can't print these, Heather, I'm sorry. We can do the artwork, but the last passes, the ones with the scented inks, are killing us. We can barely breathe. It's just toxic." I had orders to fill and needed the cash, so I put mittens and gloves on my staff and put them out in the alley with foam brushes and buckets of scented inks and ran a clothesline across my parking lot, thinking that perhaps the fumes would be less noxious, but when they were finished they all complained of dizziness and headaches, and one of them couldn't remember where she had parked. We all had what felt like a terrible hangover for another week, but I made payroll by the skin of my teeth. My stack of newspapers sat on my desk, still quiet, still crisp. On the following Monday I put them in the recycling bin.

When I told this story to Maura, she asked me if I thought that I would be happier with a partner who understood what I was trying to accomplish professionally and could be more supportive. She told me that while she believed that many successful entrepreneurs are driven by their own angst born of not being loved or supported enough as children, a partner who offered those things was crucial to one's success. I was quiet. This was where our relationship—mine and Maura's, that is—was at as much of a standstill as everything else in my life. I was working hard to stay in exactly the same place myself and was now using precious time and energy to convince her to stay there with me. She turned down the heat a bit by saying, "Look, are you getting exercise? Because with or without a supportive partner, you are still responsible for taking care of yourself, and this stress is taking years off your life if you aren't managing it."

Finally, something I could report positively on. I had been swimming again, in the river just a few miles from town during my lunch hour. I told her how I would drive my old car there, with the windows down, and walk through the brush to the rocky, then sandy beach, and then I would spend forty minutes swimming as hard as I could against the current in the deepest pool, with my eye trained on a white rock below me to keep me in the same spot. I told her how I felt stronger every day, and how much I loved the feeling of being in fresh water again and being outside, and how there was a meditative aspect to it that I had quickly become addicted to. Maura leaned in slowly, until I could see not just the top of her head but her eyes, too, which were narrowed and concerned, and asked me, "And you are just staying in the same place? The whole time?" I could hear her concern and quickly told her that no, sometimes I dove down and let the current hit my shoulders and flip me over and carry me downstream, and then I would swim back as hard as I could until I was back to where I had begun. "So, sometimes, you are going in circles," she said and then, in her most solemn voice, "Heather, you need to find a form of exercise that is not a metaphor for your life."

Months later, when there was very little left of my business, some buyers came, people who smelled a bargain and wanted to take the brand that I had built and make it into something else, something bigger and more successful. When I told Maura about it, she said to me, "Heather, this is your chance to get out." And I knew, without asking, that she wasn't just talking about my job. "I need to start building a bridge," I said, and she agreed with me, that I needed to start thinking about where I would go *when*, not *if*, I left.

But this was really just a new way to stall, because I was already thinking of my cats and wondering secretly whether, once the stress of my business was gone, John and I would have a chance. I began to picture my life without the stress of running the business, after simplifying everything and putting more focus into home. I agreed to sell my business and began to negotiate the terms. I threw myself into home improvement projects, which were where John spent all of his free time and where he was happiest. He took charge and began assigning me tasks. I spent two days pulling the old linoleum off a kitchen floor and another week pulling nails out of a ceiling. When I begged to be outside, it meant spending a day alone weeding the sorrel, which I actually thought was very pretty, in our front yard. When I told him that I thought I would be good at painting, being an artist and all, he assigned me the inside of a closet door and gave me detailed, patronizing lessons on how to do it properly. I began to see that he did not trust me to work with him on the decorative elements of our home or the projects that would allow for any creative expression. I hated the work, on my back or my knees and all the same tedious task. I didn't miss my job but I missed the creativity, the constant pushing, the excitement of a new idea, the challenge.

I thought I was doing all the right things, until I woke up one morning, just weeks before I would sign the final documents to sell my company, to find John sitting on the edge of the bed with a cat in his lap. We had spent the evening before with his family, a boisterous evening at which I'd had a very nice time, finally able to relax, knowing that I was close to a fresh start. I could tell by his face now that he had not had a good time. He had been quiet on the car ride home, but that had become pretty standard. Without looking at me, he quietly said, "I used to think that the way you acted at parties was refreshing. Now I just find it obnoxious." And then he got up and walked out of the room.

I got out of bed and put on my bathing suit, shorts, and a T-shirt. I called Wendy and told her that I was going swimming and asked her if she wanted to come. I got into my car with a blanket and a water bottle and I drove to Wendy's house, where she was waiting for me. We drove the hour-plus over the foothills and into the hot, dry valley until we reached the small highway that followed the huge river known as Redwood Creek. We followed it for another half hour until we came to the trailhead that leads to one of the prettiest and biggest swimming holes in northern California, Devil's Elbow. We hiked down the steep hill, and back and forth along an endless and precarious series of switchbacks, and then, finally, climbed over massive rocks and onto a shaded beach of thick white sand alongside a pool of water that was almost twenty feet deep and, at its widest point, nearly sixty feet across, through which ran a thick, heavy current that you could not see until it hit the rapids below, where it churned a crazy white.

I came here a lot on weekends, sometimes alone but more often with friends. I would leave my things on the beach and swim upstream against the heavy current in the clear water, with long strokes underwater that moved me just inches at a time. This river was bigger than the one I swam in on my lunch break, and deeper, more clear and wild and beautiful, and I had all day to go in circles. It would take me perhaps a half hour to get just barely around the bend, where I would pull myself into an eddy and rest briefly before I turned and dropped, underwater and with lungs full of air, motionless into the current. I could see my shadow below me, moving across the bottom of the river, so clearly that I could make out fingers and toes and long pieces of hair. I would take long strokes again, but this time they seemed to propel me twenty or thirty feet at a time because I was swimming with the current now and moving more quickly than I ever could on land, and if I held my chest very still, it was as though I wasn't even holding my breath; it was as though I was flying through a silent, peaceful space.

Wendy and I found a place on the beach to set up the two folding chairs that she had brought and settled in with our books and our complaints. There was a family near us, a mother in cutoff shorts with sad, deep eyes and thin hair. She had with her a boy who looked to be about four, a newborn baby, and a man who appeared, based on his behavior, to be the father of the baby but not the boy. Between them sat a carton of beer cans, some of which were already empty. The little boy could not or would not be still, even for a moment, and seemed only to be happy when he was scrambling on rocks or furiously digging in the sand. He moved from one activity to another quickly, losing patience or interest in everything that was not dangerous or destructive or instantly capable of getting an adult's attention. Finally, his mother put the baby down onto the towel next to her, took his hand, and led him into the water. I wasn't watching what happened next, but Wendy was, and so were the group of people to the left of us, a band of happy, naked young men, who were, I noticed, all in the process of growing beards.

The mother had pulled her little boy onto her back, with his arms around her neck, and had tried to swim across the river, at its widest point. She had made the mistake that many people do and misjudged the distance. It's very easy to do, when you are looking across a moving body of water at rocks and trees that are so massive in scale, without a house or a person there to give you a reference point. When I looked up—only because the man

next to us had stood and pointed and said, "She's in trouble!"—
she had nearly made it to the other side, but now the current had
swept her up and she could not reach the bank. She was moving
at a fast pace that I recognized as the current, though she herself
was hardly moving, her face just barely out of the water, and her
little boy clutching her shoulders and pushing her down.

I dove into the water and swam as fast as I could toward the
point, just above the rapids, where I thought I could intercept
them. The man at my left dove in, too. When I could finally see
them underwater, they were motionless. The mother's head was
completely below the surface of the water now. Her little boy
was floating behind her with just his hands still on her shoulders. He was face down but he was craning his neck so that his
forehead, his nose, and for crucial seconds at a time his mouth
could rise above water. They were exhausted and panicked to
the point of stillness now. And their eyes were perfect circles,
wide and full of fear. They were drowning. I reached them first,
and I didn't know how far behind me the man was, but I knew
that even though my arms and my lungs were stronger than they
had been when I had lived like a frog in the water behind the
schoolhouse, I could not save two people at once. I was behind
them suddenly, with my right arm around the little boy's chest,
over his right shoulder and under his left arm, moving with them
now because I wasn't fighting the current. He was holding on to
her shirt, I realized, clutching it with all of his might. I pushed
my feet forward underneath him and pulled them apart, pushing
her even farther underwater but separating them, and just as he
let go of her I saw the man reach her and pull her by the arm
toward the surface, where he expertly turned her onto her back
and hooked his arm around her chest. I had the little boy under
one arm now and was pulling him, with a strong sidestroke, back

to the beach. I spoke to him and told him that he was going to be OK, that his mother was going to be OK, but I couldn't see his face and couldn't feel him moving and wasn't at all sure that what I was saying was true, until we reached the sand and I could stand and lift him and carry him onto the beach, where I tried, because I remembered Meliah that day in her father's arms, to put my arms around him. But he wriggled free and stumbled to his mother's boyfriend, who stood with a dozen others at the edge of the water watching as the mother was pulled to shore, their baby safely in the arms of a naked stranger.

The man who saved the mother got her close enough to the beach for her to stand and then helped her, both of them clearly exhausted, walk the rest of the way to her blanket and her baby, where she collapsed. She was smiling, a broad and ignorant grin. She was oblivious to what had just happened, what had almost happened, and to what her role had been in it all. Her family surrounded her and then packed their things, and within minutes they were gone. The man who had saved the mother came over to me and thanked me and said something about how ungrateful, how foolish they were, and asked me if I wanted help finding the sunglasses that he had seen me dive in with. We swam and dove for almost an hour in the deep pool, looking for them, in silence. Finally, we gave up, and he and I shook hands, and then he put his arms around me and told me that I had made the right choice. That was when I knew that he had seen what I had done; he had seen me push the mother away from her little boy with my feet on her back, push her deeper down into the water with her lungs already empty, in order to save the little boy that she had carried into the dangerous water.

Wendy and I packed our things and climbed the hill as the sun went down, picking up the family's trail of beer cans as we went.

HOW TO
eat fresh trout

chanterelles

HAD I JUST LEFT ARCATA, WITHOUT doing what I did, I might have gone back. It would not have been enough, I know now, to build a bridge. I had to burn it to the ground behind me, too.

I had tried to go home, back to Vermont, after the incident at Devil's Elbow. I had closed the deal to sell my company and bought a plane ticket to Vermont, packed a straw hat and a swimsuit and a few thin dresses and sweaters and sandals, and told John that I was taking a vacation and that I wanted to wander around northern Vermont from swimming hole to swimming hole and see some old friends. On the first day back, I stumbled across Craig, a friend from high school. He went with me, the next day, back to the water hole behind the schoolhouse. It was one of those perfect days, sunny and cloudless, and the water was clear and cold, and I kissed him even though I knew he had a girlfriend (and, technically, I still had a boyfriend). And then I kissed him more. And then I fled, as quickly as I could, after I fought with my mother because I hated myself, and jumped into my rental car with my small bag and drove toward a friend's house, knowing that what I had done was wrong but still believing and hoping that there was another town in Vermont that would feel like home, too, where the air and the water were the same but where I could live without becoming someone I hated. But I could feel it coming up behind me, the chaos and the reckless- ness, the feeling of being eight and being hungry and poor and desperate enough to reach for the wrong branches.

I stayed with close friends on their beautiful property and swam in their pond and rested and ate and drank, but it was too far south and the water was warmer and not as clear, and while it all looked the same, it wasn't somehow. Then it was time for me to go back to California. Craig caught up with me the night before I left. He told me that I should come back, that he wanted to see me again, that he had always wanted to see me again, that I shouldn't go back to a man who didn't love me and to a place that wasn't my home. By the time I got back to John, I knew it was over. I left a few days later, moving into a spare room at Lisa and Tim's.

John didn't try to stop me, not at first. And then he broke into my e-mail account, and he found out about Craig, and he fell apart. Then he sent an e-mail to everyone I knew, per- sonally and professionally, telling them what I had done and that I was a terrible person. He and my mother became con- fidants, e-mailing each other about my every move, despising me, vilifying me together. That was the hardest part, the thing that made me realize that I had never trusted my mother, and I never would.

John soon realized how much he loved me. But we could never go back, even if that had been what we both wanted, which it never was, at least not at the same time. Had I just left, without getting involved with Craig, I might have gone back. It had not been enough, I know now, to build a bridge. I had to burn it to the ground behind me, too.

I had certainly succeeded in simplifying things. My home was a place where I was not welcome anymore. John's family, who had been like my own, was no longer a part of my life. My job was gone, replaced by a new responsibility—far from full-time—to the company that had bought my brand. After the deal closed, there was just enough money to settle the debts. I had only a few thousand dollars to my name, or about what I had begun with seven years before, when I had started the business. There was nothing keeping me in Arcata anymore, and I couldn't imagine rebuilding a life in a place where I had never felt that I belonged to begin with. My close friends, Laura and Lisa and Tim and Phoebe, Wendy and Leeann and Bill, gave me beds to sleep in, cooked me meals, listened to me cry, and then encouraged me to move on. In the end, it was easy to go.

Things with Craig imploded in the most horrible way, in that other people were hurt, too, much more than I was. My mother condemned my actions within her small town and told everyone she knew, every neighbor and every member of our family, what I had done and what I was, which in her eyes was a failure. She was clearly thrilled at being near the center of such a scandal. This betrayal hurt me so much that I couldn't talk about it to anyone without falling into anxious and endless sobbing. I cut off contact with her completely, which made her even angrier. She sent dramatic e-mails to members of our family, reporting to them what she was hearing about me, most of it false, suggesting that I was taking drugs and living on the streets, or that, possibly, I was in hiding in her town or had been kidnapped by Craig's family. This was when I realized that she had at least temporarily disconnected herself from reality, which made the entire situation more frightening. Because of this I e-mailed her and told her that I would speak to her again if she agreed to stop sending these crazy letters to our family, and if she promised to cut off all contact with John, whom she still e-mailed and even called regularly, and who had asked me to make her stop. She promised, but then, just minutes later, she accidentally sent me an e-mail meant for John. "Heather is always trying to tell me what to do," it read, "always trying to tell me how to be her mother."

The truth was that I had landed in a room in a house in San Francisco that was owned by a friend of a friend. I didn't know anyone there except my landlord, but I was within easy driving distance of my sister in Santa Cruz and my father and his sons, who were also in the Bay Area. My sister had been at my side since the beginning of the mess, defending me ferociously. My father began to tell me that he was proud of me, and, at this lowest point, I was beginning to believe him. I was traveling now between cities, helping the company that had bought my brand exhibit at trade shows in New York and Las Vegas, licensing new print designs to them as well as to a quilt fabric manufacturer and to the publisher Chronicle Books for a line of stationery. I was earning very little and living out of a suitcase, having pared down my possessions to not much more than my laptop, my ancient car, my bike, and some clothing that didn't fit me because I no longer felt hungry. Licensing was proving to be a very poor income generator, but I had signed a noncompete agreement that restricted the type of work that I could do, and I was at a loss, in general, about what I wanted to do.

I wandered around my neighborhood in San Francisco, sat in cafés with a blank sketchbook and drank wine, and sat up late watching movies, alone. Friends visited and we would talk about the previous year and everything that had happened, and they would ask me if I was alright, and I didn't know what to say. I suppose that I was, but I also was not. I was lost, and alone, and hadn't any idea what to do next, but I needed to work. I had only the smallest awareness that there was a growing interest in hand-made things, and in tutorials. I didn't yet know about blogs and saw magazines and books as the only vehicles for such work, and I knew that most of the companies that produced those magazines and books were in New York, not San Francisco. Still, I hadn't any idea of how to introduce myself.

At night in San Francisco, between trips to New York, driven to make something but too exhausted to leave the sofa, I knitted. As the summer wore on, I was still alone but less lonely, still angry but mostly at myself now, and finally able to see more clearly what had happened, where I could have done things differently, where I was doomed from the start, where I should never have been. My first project was a tiny baby sweater, just to prove to myself that now, nobody was watching. Now, anything was possible.

My next trip to New York was in August. It was muggy and I was working long trade-show days and was overbooked. I had promised my friend Tim that I would call his brother, TC, while I was in town, but the only time I had free ended up being after dinner with my aunt and uncle in Brooklyn one night, and now I was meeting him at eleven o'clock in his neighborhood, near NYU, where he had just finished attending business school. I was still dressed in the T-shirt I had pulled on after the trade show, and a skirt that was more West Coast than East Village, and rubber flip-flops, no pedicure. I hadn't really put a lot of effort into this meeting because I hadn't yet realized that I had been set up on a date. I recognized TC from a block away,

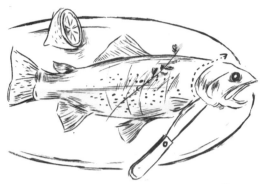

Separate head from trout by inserting a paring knife under each cheek and cutting upward.

Make a cut just in front of the tail, only through the skin, until you reach the bones. Peel back the top of your fillet. Be sure to keep the bones under the knife. Set fillet aside.

Loosen the bones by gently pulling them away from the flesh beneath them with the tip of the knife.

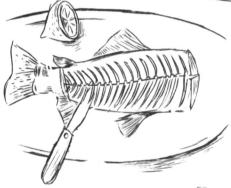

Grasp the tail and peel it away from the remaining fillet.

holding up his right hand while his left held his phone, which he had used to steer me up the correct street. He was thinner than the last time I had seen him, but his smile was the same. "The girl who can draw with her eyes closed," he said when he reached me. "Nice to finally see you again."

Drinks led to dinner the following week, another sweaty, muggy August night. He picked me up at my hotel looking polished and handsome, which made me second-guess my sundress and drip-dry hair. "I've made a reservation at a place that is supposed to be great," he said. "It's called The Red Cat." I stopped short on the sidewalk and looked at him. What were the odds, in a city with thousands of restaurants, of him choosing one my cousin used to manage and to which I once sent chanterelle mushrooms picked from the forest floor around the cabin I lived in with Mick in Arcata?

When the special of the evening was announced to be trout, *from Vermont*, he ordered it without even listening to the rest of the list or paying any attention to the way that it would be served, and when it arrived whole, fresh from the pan with head and tail still intact, a single glassy eye staring up at him from the plate, he was more than slightly surprised.

"Do you have any idea," he asked me, "how to eat this thing?"

"Yes," in fact. "I do."

HOW TO
begin again

EVERYTHING HAD ENDED AT ONCE. My grandparents, my aunt Jane, and my uncle Mike had died in the space of less than three years. Mike died in his sleep, sick with the flu in the middle of February, his body thinned and wrecked by drugs and the events of his own hard life. Jane had died of cancer even though she convinced us all that she would beat it. When she was gone, there was no one to come and sweep out The Red House, and dry it out with the cookstove, and hang the sheets on the clothesline, and put them back onto the little rows of beds, smelling like fresh hay. The house became cold and damp and quiet without her. The land in Vermont, including The Red House and the old dome site, almost a thousand acres in all, was put up for sale.

My sister and I and Jane's children did not want to see it go, especially after we had spread Jane's ashes there. My mother, who had moved into a house in town after both of my grandparents died, needed the money. My uncles seemed ready to let go of the land, too, convinced that it was too far away from where they lived. My cousins and I couldn't understand why this seemed so easy for them, why they didn't see what this place had represented to all of us. For Jane's children, it was partly about maintaining a connection to their mother. For Christie and me, it was about wanting to hold on to the closest thing we'd had to a childhood home, a place where we had never felt entirely welcome but had, nevertheless, come closest to feeling like part of a family. I had long held on to the idea that someday the property would belong to my cousins and my sister and me, that we would find a way to share it equally, that it would be a place where we would come with our own children.

When the property was sold, I tried to explain to TC how I felt. He had grown up in northwest Indiana, in a big, close Irish Catholic family, and while he had happy memories of running and playing in the woods behind his various homes, it was his parents and his siblings that he felt connected to. The homes and the towns that they had lived in didn't seem to have a hold on him. When he talked about home, he was referring to his parents' house, wherever that might be at the time. They seemed to move around a lot, as a reaction to their growing and then shrinking household. He had been raised with limited resources, too. His father had been in graduate school for much of his early childhood, and his mother had fed five children on as little money as possible. TC was a good student and a very good swimmer. He started competing as a child and chose the most challenging and least popular of race categories: the 500-meter butterfly. Swimming, with its endless, punishing practices, taught him unending endurance, patience, and persistence. He was offered several opportunities and scholarships, but he made the decision to leave the U.S. National Swim Team that he had joined in his last year of high school and go to Notre Dame, even though it wasn't one of the schools that had offered him an athletic scholarship. He did this because his parents had taught him that a good education was more important than anything else and because his family had a history there. His mother went back to work, having just finished the job of raising five children, to pay the tuition. I asked him, when we went to visit his parents for the first time and were driving on what I assumed was a familiar road to him, if he felt as though he were home. "These roads didn't even exist when I was a child. I would be lost right now if I didn't have this GPS." I thought this was sad, but he assured me that it wasn't, and when I saw what happened when we walked into his parents' little house, when I saw the tears in his mother's and sister's eyes, I understood why.

TC's family is remarkable. I've spent days with them, with both parents and a few other siblings, when almost everything has gone wrong. Just getting these people out the door with their purses and coats and children and car keys is a feat. Their father has learned to stay out of it entirely and will sit, in his pajamas, on the sofa reading the newspaper until the rest of them are literally beginning to get into the car, and then will disappear for a moment and reappear behind the steering wheel, not adding a second of delay to the outing. But then someone will have to use the bathroom, and even though that someone is an adult, this will be immediately addressed. And then we will get to where we are going, hours late and already exhausted, and someone will need to eat something, and then there will be a movement toward a restaurant, where allergies, intolerances, and special diets will need to be accommodated. The group will begin to grow as friends and other vehicles appear, and then, inevitably, the exodus of siblings and friends and vehicles and children will begin without everyone knowing, and somebody will be left behind at the Dairy Queen, without their shoes or their wallet or their cell phone, and will have to walk the four miles home. And just when I, as an outsider, think that it couldn't possibly get any more complicated or frustrating, TC's mother will pick up the phone and call the one sibling who isn't there that day and will recount the entire outing as one of the most perfect, most love-filled, most wonderful days that the family has ever shared, and then she will pass the phone around to everyone, and everyone will agree that, yes, this day was perfect because—and I have heard this phrase over and over again—"we were all together." And for someone like me, for someone with a family like mine, this moment feels like a gift.

I went to New York to live with TC in an apartment in Chelsea a year after leaving Arcata. We had been together since our dinner at The Red Cat, and I loved him and trusted him very much. He was working uptown, so every morning I walked him to his train and then bought a coffee at Penn Station. I would peruse the magazine racks, now bursting with DIY and craft titles. I was designing fabric for a company called Free Spirit, and through them I was introduced to the work of Denyse Schmidt, who had just written a book about quilting. I went, with Kim Canfield, to her book signing at Purl SoHo. Joelle Hoverson, the owner of Purl, was also there. She was opening a small quilt shop down the street and had just ordered my line of quilting fabrics from Free Spirit. "Have you ever thought of writing a book?" she asked. I hadn't, not really, but I was flattered. "You should meet my editor, Melanie Falick. I think she's the best." Joelle connected Melanie and me through e-mail and, largely because of Joelle's recommendation, Melanie asked me to submit a proposal, which became my first book. Melanie suggested that I start a blog, and, for the first time since selling Munki Munki, I felt as though I had a job.

TC was supporting me financially and otherwise. I cooked our meals, kept our house, and learned to make martinis. It was not what I knew, not what I had come from, and not where I'd ever thought I would be. Surprisingly, it was during this period of time—when I was playing the role of the traditional "wife"—that I was also able to focus on my art and design work and find the footing for a new career. When I told TC that I believed I could build a new business of my own, he told me that he believed it was possible, too, but that if it didn't work, it didn't matter, that we were a team, that he was proud of me, and that he loved me. Even if I didn't earn a penny, he wanted me to be an artist because it seemed to make me happy.

When TC asked me to marry him, I said yes, even though I didn't know what that meant, even though I had never before lived in a house with people who wanted to be married to each other. The loudest voice was coming from the place in my brain where instincts are hatched and where faith lives, and it was saying, *Yes, this is different than anything you have ever known, and this is something you should do.*

Our wedding was in Vermont, at Blueberry Hill Inn, which sits high in the southern Green Mountains, above a sweeping view of soft green hills and pastures. It was a hundred miles south of where I had grown up but at a high elevation, which made it feel much farther north. The hayfields looked, even smelled, the same. The inn was similar to The Red House, with its crooked floors and stone thresholds and narrow stairs. I wore a pale blue dress made by hand by a woman whose studio was just a few blocks from us in Chelsea, from a bolt of silk faille that I had found at Mood Fabrics. I carried wild white roses and had a cake I designed that looked like it was covered in birch bark, with wild strawberries and more wild roses made from marzipan covering it.

Planning the day had not been easy. I had not grown up imagining a wedding and was searching for ideas that seemed genuine and fitting. I had seen an image in a magazine of something another bride had done, a twinkling string of lights strung between trees, with photos of her and her husband throughout their lives clothespinned to it. I had asked my family to send me photos, whatever they had, but was met with grumbling, sad responses by almost everyone. "I'm not giving you any pictures," said my mother. "I won't ever get them back."

"Chris has all of them," said my uncle Halsey, referring to his brother. "Ask *him*."

My aunt gave me a few photos, not originals, all of them printed on cheap paper and trimmed unevenly. They showed my family at The Red House, and swimming together, and lined up on a wooden porch. I knew that if I tried to hang them from a string of lights that they would curl and look awful, and there were so few of them that it didn't seem worth trying.

The wedding photographs themselves are beautiful, especially the one of TC's family, which took almost forty-five minutes to organize and caused me to have a panic attack about dinner being late and cold. My friend Louisa watched the whole thing, trying to help, and likened the experience to herding cats. Someone kept wandering off to get someone else, and then that someone else would appear and then realize that they had left their something somewhere, and on and on and on until we had absolutely everybody, almost thirty people in all.

The picture of my extended family, by comparison, took

only a moment, I think because we were all desperate to have it over with. I sent one bridesmaid cousin up the hill to gather everyone and then down they came, in an uneven line, together but apart. We stood in odd groupings, looked straight ahead, and smiled when we were told to. When I look into the faces in that image, I am instantly reminded that my wedding day was, by sad coincidence, the day the land my grandfather had purchased back in 1960 was officially sold and was no longer ours.

It seemed that I could not get my own family to see what I saw, to imagine what I had just begun to let myself imagine, to trust that, after perhaps too many rounds of failure, I could manage something permanent, lasting. The thing that had changed in me, though, was that I no longer needed them to tell me what was possible. I had never imagined my own wedding before it was time to plan it. I had not pictured the dress or the cake or the groom or the invitations. I had not imagined the honeymoon, which was in Switzerland, hiking in the Alps, and in Italy, swimming in a perfect pool on the edge of a lake, surrounded by steep mountains. And yet here it was, all of it born out of my own hands, with the handmade invitations and the bespoke dress, and the husband, who, just like Canfields years before, had appeared out of nowhere and saved me from my own pictures of what a family was and convinced me what it could be.

Instead of twinkling lights strung between trees, we had a bonfire in the meadow the night before the ceremony. When everyone had gone to bed, I used a stick to push the hot coals apart so that they would die out more quickly, and when the flames rose up one final time before dying out completely, I looked away so that my eyes wouldn't sting, and in that instant

I saw the inn and my wedding tent and empty chairs lined up in the meadow, all under the stars. At that moment, I only saw how perfect it all seemed and nothing else, and I knew that I was ready to begin again.

HOW TO
have faith

THERE WAS A PIECE OF ADVICE THAT came to me when I was too young to understand or appreciate it, from a woman who was wise and old and whose face remains in my memory but whose name does not. She told me that no matter what I did or did not do, there would be only two things that I or any other woman would never, ever regret: "A swim, and a baby." I understood the swim part perfectly, having grown up in a damp swimsuit, and knew that late-afternoon sun and finally-dry-again hair could trick you into thinking that you did not need another jump-in, when in fact you always do. I had learned long before that if I jumped in with the faith that once I was underwater, the reason I had jumped would be clear, there was no point in arguing with myself.

For almost two decades I had shared that advice, with an assuredness that I'm certain was, at times, a little annoying, within the private confines of every "should-I-or-shouldn't-I" conversation with friends who were facing the important, life-changing decision to have children. My faith in this advice had been unwavering, unbending, and, apart from my commitment to swimming in anything, conveniently untested. I must admit that once it was me in the should-I-or-shouldn't-I spot, that faith became a little shaky. That's not surprising. It is rare that I have found faith in anything, which is too bad, because having faith in something is a very good thing, if only because it provides a rest from overthinking and indecision.

In my first few years of marriage, I felt the need for a little more than blind faith to push me past what was a very happy and comfortable stage of my life, and a little more faith that having children would not leave me in a state of regret. And this, in a very roundabout way, is why I agreed to jump into the ocean at Coney Island on New Year's Day. Because sometimes you have to test faith in order to find it.

"Regret" might be too strong a word for what I feared having children would bring. It was really more of an anxiety about the idea that my life would be irreversibly altered and filled with many new opportunities to make terrible mistakes, just when I felt like I had finally gotten the hang of things. My swimsuit and my hair were dry, so to speak. New York had granted me new, glamorous, confident friends who argued that a baby would ruin them because they would no longer be able to dress up and stay out late and travel on a moment's notice to exotic places. In contrast, a baby would actually justify my ideal evening routines, which, at that time, involved a string of Tuesday nights eating an entire bag of chocolate-covered, peanut-butter-filled pretzels while watching *The Biggest Loser*. But even so, I was suddenly good at my life. I'd become a pretty good cook, a pretty good friend; I loved my husband and my pets, and when I was in my kitchen and my dog was sleeping on his little rug under my feet and music was playing, things felt pretty complete—and, finally, peaceful. Why fuck that up?

There was also the issue of my devoted husband. TC found himself reminding me, far too often, that I was no longer going it alone. This was taking some getting used to on my part. New Year's Day was no exception. When I imagined TC's reaction to my wanting to join the Polar Bear Club at their annual Coney Island swim on New Year's Day, I pictured him being supportive and perhaps coming along as a spectator but not being crazy enough to jump in with me. Crazy was my hobby, not his. And besides, I already had definite plans to borrow the extremely warm Muppet-like fur-lined knee-length four-inch-thick warm-up jacket that he had worn between practice laps as a competitive swimmer in college and that now hung in our closet. I also planned to use his Thermos, which was better than mine, and was counting on him, post-swim, to order my favorite wonton soup from Grand Szechuan and to reward my bravery by giving me the corner of the sofa and the remote control for the day, if not the week. When I saw myself in the water, I saw myself alone. Still, even now, I always saw myself alone. So, when TC (and our very adventurous friend Stephen, who had first broached the idea) jumped at the chance to join me, I was a bit floored. "OK," I finally said, "but I get to wear the jacket."

TC not only gave me the jacket but also let me wear the pair of sheepskin boots that we shared when we took turns walking the dog. I had my warmer-than-warm Manitoba mittens, a very good hat, and a huge Thermos of hot coffee. Under another layer of fleece tights and a wool undershirt, I wore a bikini. When we stepped out into the bright, cold New Year's morning (sunny, but well below freezing), I surveyed TC and Stephen. They looked sporty and well layered, almost as though they were headed out for an après-ski fondue. I was taking no chances, making no allowances for fashion, and, as a result, I looked like I had woken up in the coat closet the morning after an ill-fated party at the Notre Dame swim team's squalid off-campus house and made a run for it … but not before stopping for coffee.

The most surprising thing, upon reaching the pre-swim party on the Coney Island boardwalk, was that so many other people were there. I had pictured dozens of people running into and out of the water—not hundreds. There was live music and a wide variety of costumes, a "strong man" demonstration, and much beating of bared chests. An adorable troupe of water ballerinas in big, flowery bathing caps and goggles fluttered about, giggling to stay warm, while a group of burly bearded men, one of them holding an enormous American flag waving madly in the wind, passed around a teensy flask. This was not at all what I had expected. I guess I had pictured a dozen or so sturdy old men espousing the health benefits and logic of cold-water swims. Isn't that what I always see on TV on New Year's Day? Instead, the costumes and mock pageantry made it suddenly apparent that everyone agreed that this was a seriously insane thing to do. And yet, we were all giddy. Everyone seemed so different, but everyone seemed to belong. It was so cold that it hurt a little to inhale, and my speech was impaired by a frozen chin. Loud music was being played for people who were dancing to stay warm. I just jumped up and down, and panicked a little inside.

When the happy mob finally moved onto the beach and the countdown began to the one o'clock call to jump in the water, we made a plan. Genuinely afraid of losing sight of each other and the pile of warm clothing we would be leaving on the beach, we mapped out our route. We were maybe fifty feet away from the water and directly between the large burly team with their American flag and a very permanent-looking wooden lifeguard stand, and we decided that it would be those two things that we looked for when coming out of the water. Confident that we would be able to beeline in and out, we shed our clothes and, when the buzzer rang, ran straight into the ocean.

TC was in the water first, almost completely submerged. He was turned around and dashing past me before I was knee-deep in the water and then gone, engulfed by the screaming crowd that was still rushing toward the surf. Stephen and I were in and out almost as quickly. The water didn't feel too bad. The air, on the other hand, was bitter. I had no water shoes on (it was difficult enough to find a bathing suit in January with a hangover), and my feet began to ache immediately. I looked at Stephen. His eyes were very, very wide. And panicked. He had just realized, moments before I would, that the wooden lifeguard stand had been moved. "WHY?" he screamed at me from mere inches away, his eyes wild, "WHY WOULD THEY MOVE THE STAND?" It wasn't a rhetorical question as much as a demand for a new plan, ideally set forth by whoever had moved the stand.

We were suddenly completely disoriented, standing on a very crowded beach that looked the same for a hundred feet in either direction, packed solid with cold, wet, and equally disoriented people. We ran a few feet in one direction, then a few feet in another, and then back again. We were not calm, nor were we able to think constructively. As many times as I told myself that I needed a new plan, that thought process was interrupted by a part of my body screaming at me to make it warm. Each time Stephen and I collided, which is what happens when you run in tiny circles with a friend and you are both in shock, we would repeat-scream at each other. "WHY? WHY DID THEY MOVE THE STAND?" or "$%@!" That was it. I believe I had the opportunity to repeat these two phrases five, maybe six, times before I turned around for just a second and lost sight of Stephen completely, finding myself alone with no one to scream at. My entire body was bright red, except for my hands, which were a sickly gray-blue, and my feet, which hurt too much to look at. I could not think in what direction, other than toward the water, I should run. I was completely and utterly incapacitated and I knew, based on the expressions of almost every member of the confused and panicked mob I was a part of, that I was not the only one. And here is where I will admit, ashamedly, that I was not thinking about TC at all. In fact, when a small opening between bodies allowed for a split-second glimpse of him, it registered as an illusion.

It was actually the long coat, flapping in the wind high above the crowd, that caught my attention. TC stood, bright pink and shaking, wearing only his tiny wet Speedo and bright orange water shoes. I knew that he could not see me; his glasses were off and his eyes were closed against the cold. He was stretched tall, with his arms high above him, each of his hands clenched tightly around the end of a sleeve of the jacket, its gold fur lining bright against the sky. It flapped and waved like a huge flag, as he must have known it would, and while I couldn't hear him, I could tell by the way his mouth moved that he was shouting my name as loudly as he possibly could. When I reached him he was so cold that he could barely manage to put the jacket around me, much less get himself dressed in the warm clothing that lay in piles next to his feet. He had been standing there for many long minutes, each of which must have felt like hours, and rather than take even a moment to put on his wool sweater and mittens and long underwear, much less to steal my sheepskin boots, he had turned himself into a bright pink, flag-bearing human beacon. There was my husband, my family. And there was my faith. I wasn't in this alone anymore. And a dry swimsuit is highly overrated.

HOW TO
not turn into
your mother

MY MOTHER HAD CONVINCED ME, FROM an early age, that children were a burden to be balanced between other, more rewarding pursuits and responsibilities. I have come to believe, actually, that among my generation of American women, born in the 1970s, I am not alone in this experience.

So, when my mother was convinced by her parents, following the fire in the schoolhouse, that she should give us up, send us to live with our father, and pursue her own life—another marriage, her own financial independence—it felt as though something inevitable had finally happened, after a long, slow wait. We went to live with our father in Virginia. My mother moved to Colorado and became engaged, but the groom changed his mind a few weeks before the wedding date. Our mother called us and told us that he had decided that he didn't want to be an "instant father." She was heartbroken, I think, and moved to France to live with an old classmate, who was also divorced. She stayed there for a winter, until she tore apart her knee skiing and was forced to come back to the United States for medical help. By then my father had decided to move to California and wanted

217

to take us with him. My mother moved back to Vermont. I went back to live with her when I was in high school, but my sister stayed with our father, visiting my mother and me during summers but for shorter and shorter stretches of time.

When my sister had her own children, in our early twenties, she told me that she could not understand how any mother—or our mother, specifically—could ever give up her children. I believed, and still believe, that this was a choice that my mother always regretted, and I even sympathized with her and with how difficult her life had been raising us alone. I also knew, though, that this action of sending us away had drawn a line in our lives between when we had a mother and when we did not, when we had been a family and when we had not. I did not, however, understand the weight of what she had done, or the impact that it had had on me, until I was pregnant with my daughter. Or, rather, until I realized that the baby in my belly was a girl, not the boy that, for reasons that were completely unfounded, I was certain I was carrying.

So certain was I about my baby's sex that I waited until I was five months pregnant to find out for sure. When the sonogram tech said it out loud, that I was having a girl, I was so shocked that I lost my balance and nearly fell off the narrow table I was lying on. This belief, that I was having a boy, had given me some peace of mind in what had been, for me, a frightening pregnancy. As far as I could see, not having had any of my own sons, but having dated and lived with a lot of other mothers' sons—and now having even married one—my only real responsibility in raising a son of my own would be to convince him that he was without fault, that he was perfect, and that no woman would ever be good enough for him. Kim Canfield, who had both a little girl and a little boy, had told me, "Have a boy, Heather.

I chase my daughter around the house, saying, 'Love me, love me, love me!' like a crazy lady and her house cat, but my son wants to live in my lap and touch my cheek and hold me, and tell me how much he loves me. Have a boy." Twin girls was what my mother had. And that was what she was burdened with and what, finally, she had let go of.

I was forty when I became pregnant. My mother and I lived on the same coast, but I saw her, at best, once a year. She and I struggled to make it through a twenty-minute phone call without one of us cursing the other and hanging up. While I tried to stay in contact with her and to acknowledge dates like birthdays and holidays, she complained to me and to other family members that she was always being kept at arm's distance from my sister and me, as though there was some sort of conspiracy against her that included her brothers and her ex-husband. It was partly true; my sister and I were, by now, in much closer contact with our father and our uncles than we were with her, but she was also becoming noticeably paranoid. When we had good news, we brought it to people who could be genuinely happy for us, which she didn't seem capable of, and when we had bad news, she had proven, again and again, that she could not be trusted with it and that helping us was not instinctive for her.

She had been living alone for a quite a while and was spending long winter hours in front of cable news, and she seemed to thrive on bad news in the way that people in small towns sometimes do—the more scandalous, the more horrific, the bigger the distraction from her own problems. My problems were of special interest to her. She was desperate to be informed, desperate for something to tell people about me, something that she knew and nobody else did. Once, when I had asked her for financial help, she had turned me down with a rude, dismissive response and then immediately written a lengthy e-mail to other members of our family, telling them that I had asked her for money, that this was proof that I "was not doing as well as I claimed to be," that she "couldn't believe anything I told her." I was humiliated and furious. What other mother would do this? I couldn't think of one, except perhaps her own. Where was this instinct that other people's mothers had, to build us up, to add value to our lives, to care for us and to defend and protect us? There seemed to be something missing inside of her, something that had been missing in her own mother, who had handed her daughter off to nannies and boarding schools for months at a time, whom I had never seen embrace or even hug my mother, who had never hidden her own disappointment in my mother. Was this a learned fault, or was this genetic? Was this something I could overcome or was there something missing in me, too, that would make it impossible for me to love, to instinctively protect, my own daughter?

Following every appointment with Dr. Berm, our obstetrician, TC and I would eat at a French restaurant in midtown. We could walk there from the doctor's office, even when I was huge, and the food was perfect for pregnancy: rich, hearty, celebratory. We went there on the day we found out that we were having a girl. TC ordered champagne and I ordered club soda, but I reached for his glass as soon as it hit the table. As I sank into my chair, muted by shock and a tidal wave of anxiety that would not subside, I felt certain that he looked happier, more relaxed, and more relieved than I had seen him in months. He had been carrying his own burden, believing that he would be having a boy, secretly worrying that he was not equipped to teach a boy how to be a good man. But he, unlike me, was an organized overachiever and accepted challenges with a courageous attitude. In other words, he had been reading thick books about the subject.

To make matters worse, I had no real birth plan, apart from feeling certain that I wanted drugs for the pain and that I was willing to pay for a plush private room. TC pointed out that my choices sounded very similar to my vacation plans when my back went out two days before we were leaving for a nonrefundable stay in Mexico. We knew that we wanted to have our baby at NYU. Dr. Berm lived, literally, across the street, and I liked the idea of being able to call him on his cell phone, the number for which he had accidentally given me. I liked Dr. Berm, even though he was known for his brusque manners and controversial politics. At one of our initial meetings, before I was actually pregnant, I started to tell him how I felt unsure about having a baby, about whether I would be a good parent or even wanted to be a parent, until he put his hand up to stop me. "I don't care," he said. "But you are not young, so figure out what you are going to do and then tell me, then I will make it happen."

"But that's it," I said. "I don't know what I want to do!"

"I didn't ask you what you wanted to do," he said. "I asked you what you were going to do."

This directive, this move of taking my actual feelings about my ability to be a parent completely off the table, was immensely refreshing. "I believe I'm going to try to have a baby," I began to say to my friends, avoiding the words "like to" and "want," and they didn't seem to notice anything was missing.

And then, when I was pregnant, Dr. Berm asked me whether I was planning to have an epidural. I pretended for a minute to be undecided, until he swatted me on the knee lightly and said, "Don't be a hero." I loved him. Also, in his spare time, he baked his own versions of all five types of Girl Scout cookies. He was perfect. He told me to go online and register on the NYU website, and when I did I saw that the only way to get a guided tour of the hospital was to register for Prepared Parenthood class. We had waited too long to sign up for the weeknight classes, which were sold out, and had no choice but to take a weekend course, all day Saturday and all day Sunday. When I told Dr. Berm our plan at our next appointment, thinking he would be impressed with my dedication to this upcoming event, he said to me, "OK, if you want, but please don't actually remember any of the information they give you when you are in labor, and if you do, don't repeat any of it to the delivery nurses. It'll just piss them off."

I waited until I was five months pregnant to tell my mother that I was having a baby. "I'm calling with some news," I said. "God, what?" she responded, sounding hopeful for something juicy and terrible. She could be counted on to be sober and in good spirits until late afternoon, and I timed my calls accordingly but always braced myself. The death of her parents and of her brother, my uncle Mike, who had been gone for almost five years now, and the sale of the land had left her in a raw and scattered state that I still hoped she would recover from, eventually. She seemed to want to talk only about tragedies and bad news and would complain to me that my sister never called her and that nobody ever told her anything, or included her in any of their lives.

I cut her off as she began to tell me something I did not want to hear. "I'm calling with *good* news," I said, starting again as though she might not recognize it as such.

"What?" she said, her tone urgent, almost desperate.

"I'm going to have a baby," I told her.

She let out an exhale, then, sounding exhausted from the three seconds of suspense and relieved but not happy, she said,

"Well it's nice to hear some good news, because I've been following this massacre? In Arizona? With the congresswoman who was shot in the head by that lunatic? It's just god-awful." I forced myself to give her a few details calmly, including the due date, then got off the phone as quickly as I could. She sent me an e-mail the next day that said, simply, "I don't have any advice for you. Everything is different now than when I had you. I hope that you'll let me see my grandchild sometime. Your sister won't let me see her kids."

I spent that whole day in bed, with a hand on my stomach, terrified.

The next day I called my father, who was genuinely thrilled for me. This gave me new hope and motivated me to get dressed and walk to the bookstore, where I bought a stack of books about pregnancy and newborns. They sat next to me, in a neat pile, on the table. Every few days I would try to pick one up and read through whatever chapter seemed relevant to me at that stage, but I would instantly feel such a bitter anxiety beginning to grow out of the pit of my stomach and into my chest that I would have to put the book down immediately and reach for the remote control. I watched episode after episode of *16 and Pregnant*, each one filling me with a sense of competence that no book could provide.

Being prepared was not what I was good at. I had become an expert, though, at managing the chaos and crisis that came out of being unprepared. Perhaps that's why I felt so out of place from the moment I walked into the Prepared Parenthood class, which was held in a large, low-ceilinged, windowless room. The air felt so still, so air-conditioned and artificial, that breathing it in felt wrong, especially for a pregnant woman. I'd like to think that what happened next was due to the lack of oxygen, but TC told me later that he had me pegged as a flight risk from the minute I sat down in the metal folding chair and began trying to look as though I were listening. I made it through the swaddling and bathing lessons, and I actually enjoyed the overviews of epidurals and other pain relief options. It was the movie that got me in the end. It was maybe a decade old, just dated enough to make the clothing the real-life moms wore distracting and to dim my confidence in it in general. The movie followed each of them through pregnancy and birth. There was a slight single mother for whom English was, at best, a second language, and a young married woman who had clearly planned every step of her adulthood and transition into parenthood exactly as it was now happening, down to the practical sports bra that she wore during her labor and the practiced breathing that she executed in a camera-friendly style. "I'm just so thrilled that this stage of my life is finally beginning," she said, as though she had been moving toward nothing but this for her entire existence. A third couple clearly hadn't done anything exciting enough to justify a lot of screen time, which was too bad since they seemed more interested in the epidural than the baby they would be having, and I had pegged them as the ones to watch.

As all three women moved simultaneously toward birth, I grew increasingly anxious. Then came the scene where the tiny single mother got helped into the bathtub during labor, smiling widely for the camera. Her own voiceover, recorded after the fact, gave us a step-by-step narration of what was happening on the screen. Her voice was tiny and odd. Her accent made it necessary for there also to be subtitles. She was using the word "contraction" over and over again, and each time she would pause before the word came, and then say it loudly and quickly, as though she had been practicing it, but every time she said it wrong. Every time, she said "constraction." The first time, I giggled; the second time, I laughed out loud. The third time, I began to realize that I was losing control. The pregnant couples around me, all ten of them, began to look my way. The room was dark, but now my inability to stop laughing was apparent to everyone. I wanted to stand, to leave the room, but I was paralyzed. Every time I thought I was recovering, she would say the word *again*, and I would explode anew. TC looked at me with a puzzled, expectant grin, as if to say, *OK, we get it, you think it's ridiculous, now pull it together*. But I couldn't. It was the movie and the ridiculous pronunciation of this horrible, frightening word, and it was the lack of oxygen, the lack of a supportive mother, the lack of anything that felt like joy surrounding this inevitable event. It all came out, right there, in that dark, windowless cavern of a room. It was a full-blown anxiety attack, manifested as uncontrolled laughter that now was making it difficult for me to breathe. My teacher misunderstood and thought that I was crying. I heard her, from across the room, say, "Yes, it's all very emotional for some people." When I was finally able to move, I went to the ladies' room and sat on a toilet, closed my eyes, and tried to imagine being somewhere else.

I had picked a name for a son but hadn't given any thought to naming a daughter, and in my final months of pregnancy, I was barely able to make even the simplest of decisions. We found a name while sitting in the Irish pub around the corner from our apartment. TC had downloaded an app that listed, by region of origin, every known name that had ever been used. He was reading through the beginning of the list and came to Beatrix. I burst into tears, literally. "That's it, that's what we are naming our daughter, that's the name," I practically shouted. "It's perfect! Nobody in Beatrix Potter's family believed in her, and she loved nature and she played with small, dead animals, and also Kerry Canfield had a Beatrix Potter address book. Don't you think it's perfect?" I said.

"Well, when you look at all of these points that you are making," he said, "how can I argue?" I knew that he wasn't sold, but I wasn't leaving much room for discussion. "Beatrix it is," he said. "Beatrix it is." I would say the name over and over in my mind and think of all the reasons that it was the most perfect one, and I would feel a little better, slightly more in control.

I was due on July 26, which would have been Mike's birthday. On what would be my final appointment with Dr. Berm, on July 20, he examined me and said, "Don't go too far from a cabby-friendly neighborhood." Then there was nothing but waiting for ten days. The weather grew overly warm, in that muggy, slow way typical of New York summers. On the morning of July 30, I got an e-mail from my mother. "I'm tired of waiting around for you to call, so I'm unplugging my phone and I'm leaving my house for a while." I turned off my computer and my phone and told TC that he was taking me out to lunch. I ate a spinach salad that could have filled a small wheelbarrow, crying as I chewed for reasons I could not explain. I was certain, now, that something inside of me was missing, some crucial part of me that should have been there, in that empty spot that, now, in these final days before I became a mother, should have held love for my own mother but instead was just a dark, empty, sad place.

Afterward, we couldn't find a cab, so I walked the twenty-five blocks home, sweating all the way. I fell asleep early that night. The next day was my mother's birthday, the only day on my calendar that was not an acceptable birthday for my daughter. My water broke at 10 A.M.

I took charge at the reception desk. "Hello, I'm checking in, Dr. Berm. This is Heather Ross. I cannot have this baby today. We need to delay this."

The nurse was staring. "You've got somewhere else to be?" she said.

"No," I explained, "I can stay here, that's fine, but I can't have this baby today. I can totally do it tomorrow, I just can't do it today." TC looked up from his clipboard, full of papers that we had already filled out online but now could not be found. His eyebrows were up but he was quiet. I realized that I was still talking, much faster now, and that I could not stop.

The nurse was no longer paying attention to what I was saying. "You've got a while yet, I'm sure," she told me as she walked away.

"That's fine," I yelled after her, interrupting my own repeating loop, "because I'm totally excited about this baby and everything, but it can't happen today!" An eerie silence followed.

I'm one of those people who responds very well to pharmaceutical drugs. They always do exactly what they are supposed to do, and I always experience side effects. The epidural that I was given (promptly, likely because somebody had put the "nut job" stamp on my chart) worked so well that I couldn't feel a single contraction. Not one bit. At one point the nurse looked at the machine with the little needle that was wagging furiously and then at me, expecting me to scream. I was texting and eating half of TC's granola bar. I had relaxed, certain that labor hadn't really begun yet, that nothing would be happening until the next day, especially now that it was almost 8 P.M. So when Dr. Berm, motioned by the nurse to come quickly, sauntered into the room and examined me, he was surprised to find that I was much farther along than my snacking and lack of screaming would imply.

"Did you bring me Thin Mints?" I asked, reminding him of his promise to make me Girl Scout cookies before he had a chance to tell me that I was in the process of having the baby, which I had clearly stated was not welcome for another four hours.

He looked at my granola bar. "How about you do us both a favor and stop eating now?" he said.

"But it's not going to happen now, is it? I mean, not today, right? I can't have this baby today, Dr. Berm, not today, please not today."

Dr. Berm looked at the clock on the wall and then at me. "It's going to be close," he said.

"It cannot be today!" I repeated. "Today," I said, leaning toward him, eyes locked, "is my *mother's birthday*." Dr. Berm pulled a chair up to my bed and looked at me, really carefully. "I understand," he said, and then, "We'll do our best," nodding to the nurse. I looked at her, and she was nodding too, both of them with the most sympathetic, supportive expressions that this pregnancy had produced to date. I leaned back and handed over the granola bar, believing that I had just negotiated the situation successfully.

Beatrix was born just after 3 A.M. The nurse put her in my arms so her head rested against my chest, against my heartbeat. I had been so afraid that I would not love her enough, that I would not have the instinct to protect her, that we would not trust each other, that there was something missing in me. She looked up at me, her eyes wet and big, her tiny hands against my skin, and I realized that I had missed something so simple, so important. She loved me already, she trusted me completely, and she knew me innately. I didn't know how I would possibly be able to build all of this between us, from scratch, with no instruction, no experience of my own in mothering, or in being mothered. It had never occurred to me that I would not have to, that the work that was ahead of me would be to protect and defend what we already were. I had been so afraid that becoming a mother would feel, from the instant it began, like a burden, and that it would tear me away from my own hard-won happiness, my precious independence. I did not know that the moment I became a mother, I would stop searching for a home, for a family, because I myself would have suddenly become both of those things.

I had been so afraid to pull this innocent little person into my family that I had not realized that it would be my daughter who pulled me into hers.

Were all of these things written down in those books, the ones that I had not read?

HOW TO
make a home

IT WAS IN APRIL AND MAY, when the snow was almost entirely gone, that the kittens would appear, the very best proof of spring. Once, when my sister and I were about six years old, they were born in the bottom drawer of a dresser to Fidget, a young mother who seemed not to think they belonged to her at all. Fidget crawled out of the drawer and peered over its edge at them, in that perfectly still way cats stare at things that they have not yet deemed to be either a danger or a snack, while her babies, their eyes just wet dashes, mewed and lifted their faces trying to find her, their heads swaying to and fro and their paws kneading at the wool beneath them. My sister and I lifted her up and put her back in, again and again, until her kittens had all latched on and pulled her down into the drawer, and then she began to purr.

Plum, on the other hand, was no longer a young mother the summer I turned ten. She'd probably had a litter of kittens every spring of her life, and while she seemed to be a fairly competent, patient parent, she also seemed, by then, to be pretty over it. I had spent days the year before watching her teach her kittens to hunt. There were lessons in stalking and crouching, pouncing and eviscerating, played out with wounded mice and grasshoppers, caught and expertly corralled by Plum with one or two of her babies at a time.

But that last summer, before we were sent to live with our father in Virginia and then California, Plum seemed, for the first time, to be an old cat. It was even hard to tell whether she was actually pregnant or if her walk had just slowed and her body settled the way an old woman's would, with loose skin, rounded shoulders, a thick belly, and tired eyes. So when she did find a safe but dusty place—in a pile of mildewed hay that was meant for the garden—to have eight white kittens with black spots that looked like tiny, plump little cows, I almost missed it. When I did find her, there were already seven kittens next to her, six of them licked clean and beginning to nurse, one of them still in its little sac of water and membrane. She pulled on a bit of it with her teeth, where the kitten's face seemed to be, and it broke open. Then she pushed it away from her baby's mouth and nose and in one deft lick opened up its mouth, which is when I heard the gasp, the very first breath, tiny but strong, fill its little lungs. By the time she had finished cleaning this baby off, the next one had arrived. Plum was exhausted now, with her eyes closed and her mouth open, and was having a hard time keeping her head up for more than a few seconds at a time. I could see the newest kitten's little face, and when I pressed against the sac that covered it, I could feel its hard little nose, so I pinched it until it opened and it began to pull apart slowly. Plum's head had dropped again, and her eyes had closed, so I licked my thumb and brushed the kitten's chin, up toward the nose, pulling open her little mouth, and heard, or perhaps felt against my hand, to my relief, that telling, quick gasp.

This particular kitten would be the first one that I held each afternoon when I went to visit Plum and her squirming, soft brood, still in their warm nest of musty hay. When I picked up my kitten I would hold my thumb toward her little face, with eyes still closed for so many days, so that she would recognize me. When I breathed in her and her sisters and brothers, I could smell other things too, like the mildew in their hay and the sourness of the milk on their chins, and even a bloody, mousey odor that must have come from their mother and her nights of hunting. And when I held them up to my throat and chest I could feel them start to purr like a little switch on a tiny, sturdy motor. To hold something this weightless, this delicate and soft, that responded to my touch with such an eager and powerful affection, made my small heart ache. I could not love them enough and I felt fully loved in return.

Back then, and even today, Vermont has a reputation for not being a welcoming place. There is even an old joke about it that goes like this: A man moves to Vermont from Boston in his early twenties and raises his family in a small town. He depends on the village store for his gasoline and half gallons of milk and sees there, for twenty years, the same small group of retired old men gathered around the store's woodstove, but they treat him, even after two decades, as an outsider, barely looking at him and never speaking to him. Finally, in frustration, he says to them: "I've been coming in here for twenty years, and you've never even bothered to learn my name or ask about me or my family. I realize now that I'll never be considered, in your minds, a real Vermonter, and as much as that bothers me, I find solace in the fact that my children were born here, and they have lived here their whole lives, and you don't get to decide whether or not they are actually real Vermonters. They are, and nothing you can do can take that away." One of the old men leans back in his chair and gives him a long, pondering look, then says, "Well, sir, I don't know about that. Now, if your cat crawled into my oven and had herself a batch of kittens, would you call them muffins?"

My sister and I were the children of newcomers to Vermont, and even though we were born in this place, and made of this place, we would never grow to feel as though we truly belonged—as someone always seemed to be around to remind us that we were different. As deep and as sure as my connection was with its fields and woods and rivers, as loved as I felt by its thick green grass under my bare feet and by those impossibly delicate kittens that appeared in my sweater drawer, or in the pile of hay, the people here let me know that I was an outsider. The lasting friends I did make came from families like my own—transplanted, usually broken, or at least broke— and when I became old enough, tall enough, to need more than kittens or a swimming hole or green grass under my bare feet, the smell of hay and mud, though imprinted into my senses, became something that I wanted to escape. When I left I had no idea where I would end up, but I would not have guessed Manhattan.

Friends who knew me at fifteen and seventeen and even twenty—when all I cared about were swimming holes and cigarettes and troublesome boys with dusty cars, and I barely had the life and social skills to survive the dorms at a state college in Vermont, much less a large, sophisticated city—marvel at the fact that I now make my home in New York City, even though I've lived here since 2005. I want to tell them that it's easier here. There are jobs for artists here. This is public transportation and heat and air-conditioning. Nobody I know has to chop firewood or hold a blow-dryer to their water pipes the morning after a freeze. I am not judged by who my parents are, though I suppose many others are. In a small town, it can be easy to become consumed, or at least distracted, by what others think of you and of your family, but there is an anonymity here, at least for me, that has meant finally feeling free of that pressure—real or imagined—to be less different. This was the word that followed me around when I was a child, that clung to me. In a small town, being different meant being an outsider. Nobody uses the word "different" in New York when they describe another person. What would they be referring to? Different from what, exactly? From whom?

Unfortunately, though, New York is not a complete cure. It won't erase anything, it just overpowers the senses and distracts the heart. And almost every day, it fails you in some small way, which is exactly what happened when I walked into the Tribeca Whole Foods, dressed like every other busy Lower Manhattan working mother—in cashmere and premium denim, and practical, expensive flat boots—with a short list in my hand that included a ten-dollar bag of granola and a package of organic bacon for my one-year-old daughter. There, I stopped short with my mouth open in front of an Easter display. I cannot claim that I didn't know what would happen when I picked up the tastefully designed shoebox-size package with the solemn bunny on it, standing just below the opening in the top of the box that revealed its contents with no paper or plastic to protect them. "Timothy's Real Vermont Hay," it read, "for Easter Baskets." From Greensboro, not forty miles from where I was born. I knew what might happen, but I picked it up anyway and let every bit of air out of my lungs before I closed my eyes and took one big gasp of an inhale.

And then, standing between the Toms shoes and the Dr. Hauschka lip balm, I burst into sobbing, heaving tears.

I don't know how many of us there are, children who spent

days and weeks and whole summers in stacks of hay bales, mid-wiving kittens, and building huts and ladders, or who walked through fields that had just been cut or who spread broken, mildewed bales onto our mothers' flower gardens or pushed them into the noses of horses through barbed wire fences, or built shelters out of tall goldenrod, twisting their flowered heads together and lying underneath them in a cloud of their dusty pollen. And I don't know how many of us are left with the smell of it all still in us, even though we left. And of that number I don't know how many of us shop at places like Whole Foods, but I know that Timothy has come for us. He knows where he will find us, among expensive specialty foods and organic skincare products that are among the rewards of the success that was our way out. This Timothy, assuming he isn't actually a bunny, or maybe especially if he is a bunny, is a genius. He has taken the smell of the home that we cannot go back to, and he has put it into a pretty box that costs eleven dollars.

As much as I love the city, for at least for the first few years, it felt to me like a very unnatural place to spend a summer. As soon as The Red House sold, TC and I began to look for a country house. Not only did I feel that our family needed fresh air and a place where we could run free in nature, but like my grandfather, I felt compelled to compensate for the sense of not belonging that plagued my childhood by creating someplace grand where we could belong now.

Briar Rose was an old, faded house, left for dead but still grand on that Saturday in April when we first saw it. The woods around it had nearly swallowed it; there had not been water or plumbing or heat in it for decades. It was near a lake and even once had a view of it from a third-floor balcony but didn't anymore because of the pines. These pines had grown so thick and so tall, in order to drown out the more slow-growing hardwoods, that the ground beneath them, on almost all of the five acres around it, was thick with ferns. It was named Briar Rose already, by someone who believed it to be a Sleeping Beauty, a noble lady forgotten and caught under a spell, waiting for someone to come along and love her, and wake her up.

TC thought she looked more like a beaten down old lady than one imbued with magic, but, like me, he could also see what she could give us. We could have wood fires, we could swim in the summer and cross-country ski in the winter, we could walk in the woods with our dog and sit on our porch at night. I could cook in a spacious kitchen, and Bee would have a sleeping porch, where she could invite friends and cousins to stay up late with her. I could have my own bonfires, perfect in the moonlight, and listen to the radio while I cooked, and pick berries, and mushrooms, and flowers from my own land. It was an ambitious, expensive dream. The possibilities reminded me of my aunt Jane, who taught me that traditions need not be old, or inherited. And it was the perfect location; it was the country house but not quite the country, exactly halfway between New York City and turning into my mother.

We opened up the walls and ceilings, working carefully between the ornate woodwork, and filled them with warm insulation. We installed new furnaces and a radiant heating system through the house's floors, and replaced the plumbing and the electrical. We sanded down the old pine floors and sorted through stacks of screen and storm windows. We pulled down the highest, most opportunistic pines and saw the hardwoods begin to stretch out. We ignored the chipmunks who jumped from their branches and down our chimneys to the places that they deemed safe enough to store their collections of seeds, which for another year we would find in neat piles under our pillows. We battled mice, by the hundreds, and an overweight groundhog who barely hurried out of our way when we crossed paths on what seemed to be his front porch. Like the owl that watched us from a high branch at the edge of our forest, they all seemed to think that the house was still a part of their world, not ours. And I feared that they were right.

We finally moved in, after a solid year of renovation, with our brand-new baby girl. TC and I were exhausted, sleepless new parents who had just spent every dime they had between them to save a house and to make a place that was supposed to feel like home now, but somehow didn't, not exactly. Everything was still new and a little foreign. It would take some time for it to feel like home to TC and me. But not to my tiny daughter Bee, who slept so peacefully there from the beginning, in a cradle pulled close to my bed because her nursery felt too far away. This place, to Bee, was already home.

Bee can grow to love this place in that way that children love a place because of the way they are loved in it. The smells and sounds that seem new to me, that will probably always seem new to me, are already part of her own chemistry: the rustling of the pines when they sway, balanced on their shallow root bases; the echoing taps of the woodpeckers that come for the hardwoods when they begin to die because the pines steal their sun; the hoots of the owls that are proof that this is a safe, good place; the odors of old, musty stone walls, mountain laurel, and cut grass. She will be made of this in the same way that I am made of a different place. I can't promise Bee that Briar Rose will always be hers, because none of us can know what the future holds, not exactly, not with certainty. But now, while she is still young, I can give her a home that can, at least in my most ambitious dreams, always be hers, and that will always be—and feel—this way.

And I am determined to build a future here, as well as a past. Briar Rose is where we spend summers and holidays, and each of them brings opportunities for new traditions. We have a bonfire every summer, in late August, when there isn't any moon and you can see the most stars. For New Year's and for TC's birthday we have steak, because in TC's family there was never any money for steak. For Christmas I make a *bûche de Noël*, with chocolate bark, and for Mother's Day we take a picnic into the woods and pick tiny wild violets and daisies. For Bee's birthday, in the middle of the summer, I make a cake that looks like a beehive and I set a table for twenty-six on our massive stone porch, and our neighbors and their children come, straight from the lake with their wet hair, leaving their bicycles in a pile in our yard.

TC loves winter and Bee will probably love summer the most, but I love spring above all, and we celebrate spring on Easter Sunday, which is a wonderful hybrid of TC's Catholic upbringing and my pagan one. We pull down the storm windows, throw open the doors, and hide eggs in the woods, where tiny green shoots of grass are already appearing. For Easter this year I made Bee a chocolate rabbit with a vintage mold I found that reminded me of Mexico, of the first Easter I remember, with my sister, when we ate chocolate together while our mother slept. I left a space inside the rabbit big enough for a small gift and asked TC to find something for her, and he produced a tiny silver charm. I filled a little white basket with the short green grass that had just begun to come up around our house and with Timothy's hay from Vermont. I put the chocolate bunny inside and waited, sitting on the floor outside Bee's room in the quiet, blue light of early morning. I waited for Bee to wake up, for her spring to begin.

acknowledgments

THIS IS THE SORT OF BOOK THAT COULD NOT HAVE
ever come to be without a lot of encouragement and support.
I am lucky to have had a steady, daily supply of both from my
husband, TC Fleming, and my editor and dear friend, Melanie Falick. It's also the sort of book that I could never have
found the courage to put out into the world without my sister's
promise to love and support it without even having to read it
(because, as she likes to point out, she is my sister and that is
her job), or my father's proud encouragement, even when I am
writing about him.

Thanks also to my cousins, the most loyal and steadfast
band to which I have ever belonged, most especially to Martha
and to Jon. And to my uncle Chris, whom I love very much. I
am honored that you trusted me enough to support my writing
this book.

Thanks to my good friend, talented designer Brooke
Hellewell Reynolds, who I'm sure will one day turn out to be
my own distant cousin, because even though we could not be
more different we are also a little bit the same, and to my agent,
the incredible Steven Malk, who has taught me to value the work

I do as an artist and author, and in doing so, has given this book a happy ending.

I am very fortunate to have been born to parents who taught their little girls to be brave, to take risks, to make mistakes, and to stand up for themselves. They also taught us the most important lesson of all, which is that failure is not something that we need to worry about, it is something that happens, something that changes us and makes us better, and something that we should not be afraid of. Not ever.

And finally, to Lobo, who couldn't care less what I've done, where I've been, or where I'm going, as long as he gets a treat and a scratch behind the ear the absolute moment I return.

ALPINE HAVEN

BLACK FALLS

THE DOME

THE RED HOUSE

MIKE'S HOUSE

BEAR RUN,
VERMONT
and Vicinity